The
Smart
Spot

The Smart Spot

4 Steps to Setting Intentions and Using Intuition to Achieve Success

Dia North

Red Wheel
Boston, MA / York Beach, ME

First published in 2003 by
Red Wheel/Weiser, LLC
York Beach, ME
With offices at:
368 Congress Street
Boston, MA 02210
www.redwheelweiser.com

Library of Congress Cataloging-in-Publication Data
North, Dia.
The smart spot : 4 steps to setting intentions and using intuition to
achieve success / Dia North.
p. cm.
ISBN 1-59003-038-9
1. Success—Psychological aspects. 2. Intuition. I. Title.
BF637.S8N655 2003
153.4'4—dc21
2003013677

The Smart Spot® and Intentional Intuition® are registered
trademarks.
Typeset in Sabon and ITC Officina Sans
Printed in Canada
TCP
10 09 08 07 06 05 04 03
8 7 6 5 4 3 2 1

*This book is dedicated to
my best friend.*

Table of Contents

Acknowledgments

I would like to thank the following people for their involvement in getting this book out of my own Smart Spot and heart and onto the pages you hold in your hands.

Jan Johnson for her vision, persistence, humor, and kindness; Cheryl Kimball for her comprehension and developmental pragmatism; Ann for Katmandu and beyond; and Andrew for his strength, friendship, and strong intuition. Thanks to my friends at the Academy without whom my skills would be dull and lifeless and to everyone at Adams for their encouragement, friendship, and indulgence. Thanks, long overdue, to Ida Johnson, my 8th grade English teacher who nurtured my first work to publication, and to my family and friends for providing the impetus to always move forward.

Many thanks to everyone at Red Wheel for their sound advice, professionalism, and indispensable guidance through every phase of the book-birthing process. I wish to acknowledge the Academy of Intuitive Studies and Intuition Medicine® for its contribution to my life and work. Special thanks to Founder and Executive Director, Francesca McCartney, and Dean of the Graduate School, Michael McCartney, for some of the concepts and techniques.

The many examples of perception, visualization, and energy management in business came from true stories—mine and those of clients, friends, associates, and students. Any errors or omissions are not intentional and I take full responsibility for them.

I acknowledge the grand intention of *The Smart Spot* for its power to inspire and facilitate creative action.

• • • • • • • • • • • • • *I*ntroduction

You Are More Than You Think
(The Smart Spot Explained)

You have the ability to create everything you want.

Everything. In your life and in your work. Today.

Without any more money, more time, or earning an advanced educational degree.

This is not simply an optimistic statement. It is not the introduction to another one of those "positive thinking" books. And it is definitely not a pitch to get you to buy something (or a whole lot of somethings) to "make it work."

This book is about how to access your limitless innate ability to create what you *really* want in your work and in your life.

The only things you need to make it work are an open mind and the willingness to practice a few simple techniques until they become second nature to you. Having this creative mind-set will allow this compelling idea to help you access your creative self and ultimately transform your life.

The idea is called the Smart Spot process, and it really is about what it says on the cover—four simple steps to intentionally use your intuition to create what you *really* want.

What Is the Smart Spot?

Scientists and the medical community have believed for many years that we humans use only a small percentage of our brains, as little as 10 percent. There has been a lot of speculation and some research into what the other 90 percent could be used for: various types of genius, extrasensory perception, and so on.

If you wanted to be a very smart person—especially in one field or on one topic—you could go to school for years to learn about it. To get a master's degree or Ph.D. in the subject, you would not only go to school for many years, but you would do a huge amount of research about this topic and write a lot about it—perhaps even a whole book. After all of that, you would be tested both verbally and in written format by a panel of experts on the topic. You would know the subject backward and forward. It is possible that you would use a larger percentage of your brain than another person who does not go through such mental rigors.

But this is not the only way to become "smart," to use more of your mind than that 10 percent. Just like analytical learning (such as the Ph.D. program mentioned above), using one's intuition at a very effective level also can be learned through training. The schooling is different from a traditional Ph.D. program because it requires expanding the mind in a different way—a nonanalytical way.

To connect with your intuition is to become familiar with an area of the human mind that you may never have been introduced to previously. It is the center of your creative intuition, what I call the Smart Spot.

The Smart Spot is the command center for all creative thought and action. It represents a specific physical location in the human body, a state of mind, and a process.

The Smart Spot is situated at the hypothalamus—the endocrine gland approximately located in the three-dimensional center of your head measured from ear to ear, crown to jaw, and nose to back of the cranium. The hypothalamus is responsible for the internal control of the entire body. It regulates homeostasis in the body by producing the "controlling" hormones that regulate body temperature, hunger, thirst, and emotion among many other important functions.

When your awareness is focused on this spot, you are operating from a place of fluidity, effectiveness, and calm assurance. You truly are "smarter" because you generate a state of mind in which your intellectual analysis of a situation is combined with acute sensory perception (sight, hearing, feeling, taste, and smell) and creative intuition (instinctual awareness, wise perception, and visualization).

Drawing all of your awareness into this Smart Spot literally positions you physically, psychologically, and intellectually to accurately apprehend situations, make confident decisions, and initiate appropriate action based on the highest outcome for all concerned.

You can learn how to do this by following the Smart Spot process explained in this book. This four-step process—establishing a grounding connection, setting an effective intention, accessing your creative intuition, and acting with intention—will help you access all of your abilities to perceive, analyze, and act—responsibly, effectively, creatively.

To be able to do this takes some practice, just as it requires practice to know where the tennis ball is going to land when you hit it a certain way with the racquet. But in the end, the knowledge you gain from this book together with lots of practice will allow you to locate the Smart Spot and easily operate within the "laws" of the Smart Spot process to create solutions and ideas on demand.

We will spend most of our time together in this book understanding and practicing techniques to help you do just that. Before we talk about the specific method to access your Smart Spot, though, let's look at some present-day research and thought about the concept of energy, your energy body, and the idea that there is more to everything—including you—than you might imagine at this moment.

Energy Is the Future

It has become popular to talk about energy as this mysterious "something" upon which all events, happy and unfortunate, can be blamed. Metaphysics books explain energy in great and lengthy detail without connecting it much to our lives and work. The scientific community has its own answers. For most people, the concept of energy is anything but clear.

So why even try to understand it? Because energy is the future. Understanding and using our enormous innate creativity is the next step in human evolution. The book you hold in your hands describes the way that people are right now—how we relate to ourselves, to one another, and to our surroundings on a subtle energy level. You have not been taught to sense these subtle relationships up until now, but just as one generation's philosophy is the next generation's common sense, the basic principles stated in this book are within your grasp today and might seem elementary in just a few years.

There Is More to You Than You Think

As recently as fifty years ago Americans had almost no information about their bodies. The President's Council on Physical Fitness begun during John F. Kennedy's administration in the early sixties created a wave of exercise books, fitness centers, nutritional labeling, and RDAs (recommended daily allowances) for vitamins, minerals, and fiber. We now know quite a bit about our physical bodies. Americans have learned to significantly increase their level of health, fitness, and, ultimately, lifespan by learning how the physical body works and how to "listen" to its needs.

That was then, this is now. It is now time to expand your understanding about yourself. You are a physical body, and you are also made of energy, just like everything around you. A basic understanding of how your energy works can help you feel better, be happier, and expand your creative expression.

The Smart Spot process is based upon the inspiration that there is more to you than your physical body and your intellectual thinking ability. It is this "more"—this other aspect of you—that contains your limitless creative power. It is what has been left out of the equation in most other prosperity and intention-setting plans, and it is why this one really works.

Let's look at this idea and build a vocabulary to discuss it.

You = Physical Body + Energy Body

Every human being is born with two bodies. The structure that you call "you" is actually a collection of parts that fall into the broad categories of your physical body and your energy body.

Your physical self, the one you know the most about, is the "you" that you bathe and dress and feed. It is your corporeal being and is comprised of your arms, legs, hips, head, and other body parts. This physical structure is your "walking around body"—the one that gets you to work and onto the tennis court and enjoys a good meal.

Medicine and science provide an almost constant stream of information about our physical selves. Our knowledge of nutrition, exercise, genetic programming, and other bodily information is continuously expanding. Yet this is just one aspect of the complete "you."

Your physical body is also the home and vehicle for a collection of subtle abilities I call your "energy body." Much less is generally known about our energetic selves, yet it is just as important a part of the human anatomical system. Your energy body (also referred to as "your energy") is your quintessential self—your *creative essence*. Understanding the concept of the energy body and learning to effectively communicate with it are essential to your success in using your intuition intentionally.

What Does Your Energy Body Look Like?

Your energy body is very subtle. While a small percentage of people have a special kind of sight that enables them to see the energy body, most cannot see it without benefit of a special technique called Kirlean* photography. In a Kirlean photograph the energy body looks similar to your physical body except that it is cloudlike or filmy. It has arms, legs, a head, face, and so on.

Some people have the ability to directly view the energy body. To those with special training or born with a unique kind of "sight," your energy looks like a subtle version of your physical body. It looks like a misty or etheric version of you.

The energy body is much more than its unique appearance. It represents your *capacity to create* and at the same time *contains all of the knowledge of your ancestry including instinctual human behaviors and genetically determined traits*. With training and practice you can learn to access this creative knowledge base and use it to construct virtually anything you can imagine.

---

* Kirlean photography is a special method used to make subtle (not seen by normal vision) energies visible. In 1939 Semyon Kirlean discovered that when half a leaf was photographed using his special camera, the missing half of the leaf would appear. You may see an example of a Kirlean energy photo on my website at *www.dianorth.com*.

Does Everyone Have an Energy Body?

Yes, everyone has an energy body. Your energy is an essential aspect of the self that everyone possesses. It is the companion to your physical body and it provides a vital function, quite literally. What you have thought of up until now as "your body" is actually animated by your energy. It is that *je ne sais quoi* that makes your blood flow through your veins and thoughts move between nerve synapses, and that regenerates every cell in your body every seven years. Your physical body is a complex collection of human hardware, plumbing, and electrical responses. In a very real sense your energy body is your life. Both bodies—energy and physical—are required for you to be alive on Earth.

What Does the Energy Body Do?

In addition to animating the physical body, your energy has a wide range of creative capabilities that fall into the broad concept of intuition. We will explore this idea in detail in this book. We generally think of intuition as intuitive perception, such as advance knowing, seeing, or hearing at extraordinary levels. But intuition is much more than that.

Your inborn intuition is your ability to *create*—ideas, plans, organizations, physical objects like buildings, new inventions, and great works of art.

This book and my classes and private consultations are all about learning how to access this birthright—your natural aptitude to create virtually anything you can imagine—by gaining understanding about and learning to communicate with this creative energetic part of yourself.

What could be more exciting?

Why Haven't I Heard about This Before Now?

The idea of your energy may be new to you. You may be thinking, "If it is so powerful, why haven't I known about it before now?"

There is a lot of support and education based around language and mathematic and scientific capabilities, yet the subtle world of intuition and energy is less widely known. Why is this so?

The short answer is that humans typically learn and know only those things that are applicable to their lives at any given moment in time. In the course of human evolution, having only nodding acquaintance with our energy up until now has been appropriate. Until the past century, the world was a place where people had to struggle constantly just to survive. When life is filled with hungry tigers; marauding invaders; and unpredictable droughts, floods, and plagues, people's main concerns are general physical safety and a stable food supply. That kind of environment requires information about basic survival.

Things have changed dramatically within your lifetime. In the recent past, people in the developed world have gained more safety, more success, and more leisure time than they have had at any other time in history. This markedly less uncertain and dangerous existence opens the way for amazing new inventions and ideas. In other words, elevation of the species above survival levels has begun to allow human thinking and creating abilities to move into new areas and up to truly remarkable levels.

This exciting era of the world requires a new way of thinking. It is time to be intentional about your ability to create everything you need and want for yourself, your organization, and your community. We are intentional when we understand and commandeer our energy.

But what *is* energy? A brief discussion is in order.

Energy Follows Thought

Perhaps you have heard the expression "Energy follows thought." The idea is that at a subatomic level every person, every thought, every sound, every thing is comprised of pulsating light that is in a constant state of change. Directing that change—creating a path for it to follow—can be done through knowing what you want (thought) and clearly setting the goal (intention) for it to happen.

This is better understood now than ever before. Classical physics perfectly explained the world around us until about one hundred years ago when quantum theory unveiled a new level of reality. The quantum world is one of intrinsic uncertainty—a world of possibilities. As Francesca McCartney, founder and director of the Academy of Intuitive Studies and Intuition Medicine®, writes in her book, *Intuition Medicine: The Science of Energy*: "Physicists, mathematicians, and physicians now perceive what artists and mystics have always known: the human being is made of energy. Thoughts, emotions, colors, disease, beauty, and spirituality . . . all exist as energy."

A Down-to-Earth Example

Constant change and possibility is all around us. This is easy to see by observing the various states of water. Liquid H_2O (water) exists at room temperature. When water boils, it becomes steam, the gaseous, or etheric, version of H_2O. Freeze it and it becomes ice or snow, the solid version of H_2O. If you combine water with other elements, you get new formulas; for instance, adding a carbon molecule creates CH_2O—formaldehyde.

This ability to change appearance and functionality is a quality of virtually everything in our universe. The molecules that make up air, soil, planets, and all the cells in the human body are essentially the same. The energy that makes up our bodies and our thoughts is, at its essence, also the same. It is light vibrating in constant motion. All of us and all things are comprised of this subtle world of change.

Ours is a quantum world of uncertainty and possibility. You can either recognize this fact and let it work for you or deny it and risk its undermining consequences.

If anything can (and does) change from moment to moment, why not create the change *you* want? Of course you first need to know *what* you want, then *how* to set it into motion.

What you want to solve or to create is something that you and your organization will decide. It is part of an internal brainstorming process in which you explore your needs. It requires knowing what you *want*, not just what you *don't want*, and then believing that you (or the organization) deserve the desired thing or situation.

Intention is the energy mechanism—the vehicle for momentum—that will carry your idea forward to successful realization. The effective techniques presented in this book will help you to figure out what you really want and then how to intentionally create it.

Let's Get Started

This book is The Future. The ideas presented here are being taught to children and adults who are helping to develop the new human creativity paradigm. Mastery of the techniques described in *The Smart Spot* will one day be as commonplace as high school diplomas. And that day is not far in the future.

This book is a basic course in how to comprehend and communicate with your energy system. Your energy body is a "go with"—it is the companion structure to every physical body born on Earth. This is great news! You already have everything you need to start creating with intention today; you just need to know how to use it. And by the time you finish this book, you will.

I look forward to introducing you to your vast creative potential. This will be an exciting journey—one that will forever change your perception about how to make *anything* happen in your life and your work.

Let's get started.

. . . . *T*he Smart Spot
Process

An idea took the world by storm in 1984.

Before the 1980s, the concept of "computer" was a frighteningly huge IBM mainframe running incomprehensible "computer languages." These machines were managed by a powerful computer department, which had the final word in all matters regarding the dissemination of information.

Apple Computer, Inc. significantly expanded this idea with the introduction of the Macintosh. Almost overnight, the Mac's innovative features changed the computer industry with windows technology, icons, unlimited fonts, color, and a clever interface.

The Macintosh was definitely different—attractive and friendly. The industry pronounced it "intuitive" because it appeared to "read the user's mind" and "communicate" with him. The computer even had a human name, Mac. The word was out—humans *could* have a meaningful relationship with a machine.

The idea of a "user-friendly" computer was so exciting that it transformed everyone, whether able to type or not, into a prospective user—from secretaries to professionals and corporate executives.

Suddenly it was impossible for computer departments to control all information. Power struggles ensued, and when the dust settled it was a different world. Today nearly everyone has access to the information needed to make sound business decisions right from his or her own desk. The simple-to-use machine sitting on that desk is as likely to be imprinted with the name DELL, Gateway, or IBM, as Apple, yet it is undeniable that the ideas behind the Mac are present in virtually every computer now in use.

This is a great example of the power of well-conceived and clearly communicated intentional intuition. In the '70s, Steve Jobs founded Apple Computer with his friend, Steve Wozniak. They had a big idea about how to change the world with "insanely great products": Design computers that anyone (even a child!) can use, and everyone *will* use them to access the world of information. This will change the way people think and work. They will be empowered. They will be creative. They will be free. The idea of changing the way that people everywhere think, create, and process information is a very big intention.

This intention has been clearly and elegantly communicated over almost twenty years through innovative product design and advertising. Today the Mac is presented as a fun, powerful, effective tool that still encourages each of us to "Think Different"—to continue to evolve.

A clearly stated business intention can revolutionize an industry. And although it does seem extraordinary, when that intention is consistently stated, it can actually change the world. In truth, every person and every company can do that. All it takes is to decide what you want to create and then communicate that intention clearly, creatively, and repeatedly until it happens.

The introduction and acceptance of the Macintosh is one of my favorite business-intention stories because the idea was effective against almost impossible odds. A company that began in a garage with spare electronics parts going up against business giant IBM? Unthinkable! What is more, this upstart stood for creative thinking in opposition to traditional ways of working and processing information. Earth shattering! In the process of fulfilling its own intention, Apple has changed the way virtually every other part of the industry, and by extension all of us, works.

Intention is the difference between a great idea that creates a revolution and a great idea that fizzles. An effective intention sets a context for creative action. It helps everyone and everything involved to work toward the common goal.

This book presents effective hands-on techniques to help you set effective intentions in business and in your life. The idea is enormous—you *can* create everything you really want—yet the techniques themselves are easy to understand and relatively simple to do.

Let's take a moment to define the elements that make up the Smart Spot process before we jump into the techniques to intentionally create what you want. Knowing what you want is the key element in setting an effective intention. Knowing how to manifest it is part of your inborn creative strength called intuition.

What Is Intuition?

Intuition is your innate ability to create everything in your life— ideas, activities, relationships, and projects. It is the essence of creative expression and as such forms the energetic basis for creative acts big and small, from singing a song to inventing a new product.

Intuition is also your natural perceptive skill. It provides direct insight and is your ability to immediately sense and synthesize huge amounts of information. Business visionaries use it every day to make hard decisions. It is anything but a "soft" skill. In fact, it is an enormous advantage when creating long-term plans and deciding among complicated choices.

Intuition comes with being alive. You already have it. In the next chapter you will begin to learn how to use it with intention.

What Is Intention?

The ability to instantly sense and synthesize information, as powerful as that can be, is only as effective as the goal or purpose for which it will be used. It is this goal that I have named "intention." Intention involves *knowing* what you want, and *clearly stating* it. Intention setting is made most effective when you operate from your Smart Spot. You will learn how to do this in Chapter 3.

What Is Intentional Intuition®?

Intentional Intuition® is visualizing a goal and creating the means and momentum to achieve it. It is getting to your Smart Spot to access your intuition and then directing your intuition to achieve what you want. In the Smart Spot process, your enormous creative potential (intuition) makes an extremely powerful connection to your intuitive goals (intentions).

The Four Steps of the Smart Spot Process

There are four steps to the Smart Spot process:

1. Establish Your Grounding Connection
2. Set an Effective Intention
3. Access Your Creative Intuition
4. Act with Intention

These four steps can be viewed as hierarchical building blocks as seen in figure 1.

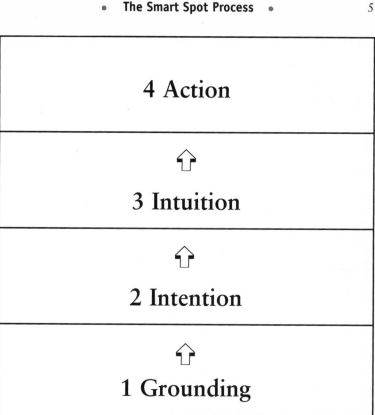

Figure 1. The Smart Spot process

The four steps are all dependent upon one another and are most effective when used in combination; however, each step is also special and important in its own right.

In this book we will devote one chapter to each of these steps. Briefly described, they are:

1. Establish Your Grounding Connection. In this step, you will learn how to get to the Smart Spot to connect to your intuition.

2. Set an Effective Intention. This chapter demonstrates how intention setting creates success by harnessing your intuition to an objective goal.

3. Access Your Creative Intuition. This chapter shows you how to "get there" and once you start receiving information, how to decode and understand it.

4. Act with Intention. This chapter explains how to act on the intuited information to bring your intention into reality.

The steps are hierarchical. They happen in order because each step introduces a skill that sets the stage for the next step. Even if you do not perceive yourself as doing them "in order," they are so interdependent that you will end up doing them in the described order no matter where you begin.

The Smart Spot process builds one step upon the other, similar to the way many of us learn to read. We first learn to recognize characters of the alphabet. This is an essential first step. Then we learn to recognize words, then put those words into sentences, and finally we learn to read and eventually to write the great American novel, an effective business proposal, or an email message that hits the mark.

Grounding is step one. It is the basic block (similar to the importance of learning the alphabet). Intention is quite literally the words. Intuition is putting those words into whole thoughts or ideas. Action is the culmination—the completed result—the novel, proposal, or email message.

How to Get There

When you are first learning a skill, consciously doing all of the steps in precise order and as closely as possible to the model or process presented is helpful because you have no independent frame of reference for learning the skill. Then, once you know enough about it to perform "without thinking," you reach an entirely different level of skill.

For example, when learning tennis, coaches admonish, "Don't think too much!" because they know that analytical processing is simply too slow to provide immediate, perfect reactions like "knowing" where the ball is going to land on your side of the net and being positioned to powerfully engage it—all within a fraction of a second.

It is simply impossible to deductively reason out every aspect that needs to be considered in that moment. Imagine all that must be processed! You must consider all the characteristics of the ball and the court: the position of the ball, the trajectory of its bounce, and the visual distortion possible from shadow or glare on the court. You will need to figure out and constantly update moment by moment your opponent's strategy, physical condition, and mental state. And you must decide what is required from you every minute— mentally, emotionally, and skillfully—to determine how much power to put into each swing, the most effective angle of your racquet when it engages the ball, and the most advantageous position for the ball to land on the other side of the net.

Whew! Imagine having to think all of that through in a split second and process a "perfect" result—one that earns you points. This is why experience and being "in the zone" are so important. It is also important in business meetings, in public speaking, in conversation, and in life in general.

When any skill has been mastered, it appears to be executed effortlessly. Most master practitioners will tell you that it feels like it is "without effort"—not because nothing is happening but because *everything* is. All that is required for supreme efficiency, beauty, and effectiveness is working as a perfect, harmonious "whole." Every aspect of the skill is being done at once—elegantly, flawlessly, flowingly.

Mastery of the skill is the key. Once proficiency has been achieved, you can "position" your mind to align mental, emotional, and physical faculties, sharpen each to its most exquisite brilliance, and choreograph them in a way that is far greater than the sum of the parts. First, however, you need a model to follow that will allow you to "get there."

So it is with the skill of using your creative intuition. This book provides such a model. It is based upon the concepts taught at the Academy of Intuitive Studies and Intuition Medicine®, where those seriously involved in energy medicine have studied for twenty years and where the author, after being granted the Master in Intuition Medicine certification, continues to teach and study in the graduate education program.

The Smart Spot process described in the next four chapters is a proven model for learning how to access your enormous creativity. Each of the four skills involved is presented in learning stages. Each of the four steps includes:

1. A description of behavior or feeling related to the skill (e.g., the feeling of knowing everything going on around you without using your eyes or ears is the mark of creative intuition).
2. The "Energy Explanation"—how the skill is described and explained in energy terms.
3. Several stories that illustrate the skill being used at various levels of accomplishment.
4. A guided visualization to help you connect to the Smart Spot and learn the skill described.
5. "Try This" and "Questions to Ask Yourself" exercises to reinforce learning.
6. A "My Intention" exercise to help you set your own goals while learning the Smart Spot process.

There is also additional support in this book and beyond for you to connect to and enhance your skills in intentionally using your intuition.

- Refer to the glossary for descriptions of unfamiliar terms.
- For extra support, see my website (*www.dianorth.com*) for personal assistance in experiencing grounding, setting an intention, or accessing your intuition.
- For support on implementing your intentions, contact one of our professional intuitive coaches for personal assistance.

The next four chapters describe the four steps required to lay the groundwork to help you locate the Smart Spot and experience intentional intuition, perhaps for the very first time in your life.

2

Step One: Establish Your Grounding Connection

Grounding is the essential first step in the Smart Spot process. It sets the stage for all successful results because it gets you into the Smart Spot to create everything you really want. Grounding is the secret to manifesting anything in the real world.

Andrew Krcik, Vice President, Marketing, PGP Corporation, talks about his experience of grounding in a former job:

> The thing I noticed most about grounding was the *physicality* of it. I found that if I got wound-up, I had done it wrong. Though there are always difficult situations in business, I found not being grounded makes them worse. When I worked in the dot.com world, the general expectation and reward was for being wound-tight. Yet when I resisted this and maintained my grounding, my decisions were the ones accepted by the rest of the executive team. Businesses should reward people for being calm because that is where

the best decisions come from. Calm is a sign of grounding, and grounding is a sign of calm.

What Is Grounding?

Grounding is the device that connects your Smart Spot, your energy body, your physical body, and the earth. When you are aligned, connected, and communicating, virtually anything you intend happens.

In a very real sense, grounding is essential to conducting life and work with purpose and intention.

Virtually any "system" designed to create prosperity or enhance creativity in all of the books on these subjects (and there are a lot of them!) cannot work without some version of this vital connection.

Grounding—the Energy Explanation

In the introduction you learned that your energy body is defined as your quintessential nature, your creative essence. Your energy body has the ability to create everything you need and want in your life. Whether this happens depends in large part upon how successful you are at keeping your energy body inside of and in communication with your physical body. Your energy body, creative as it is, operates effectively on the physical plane only when it is connected to your earth presence—your physical body. Grounding is what keeps these two parts of you connected. It also facilitates communication among your energy body, your physical body, and your Smart Spot.

Making the Connection

You will learn the specifics of how to make the grounding connection in the visualizations on pages 22 and 25. In very general terms, it is simply a matter of accessing your Smart Spot and imagining that you're pulling your energy body *into* your physical body and attaching them at the base of your spine as shown in figure 2. Then

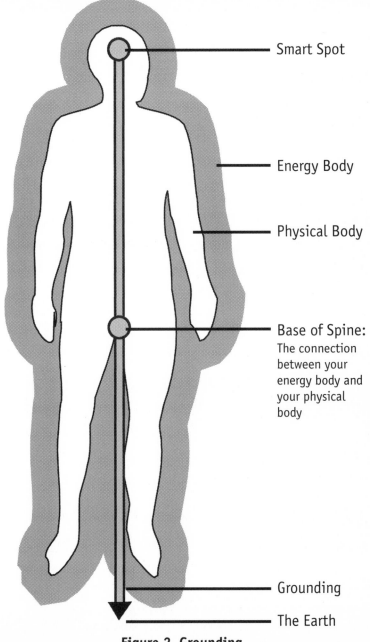

Smart Spot

Energy Body

Physical Body

Base of Spine:
The connection
between your
energy body and
your physical
body

Grounding

The Earth

Figure 2. Grounding

you imagine a line of energy extending from the base of your spine into the center of the earth. Grounding, then, is the process of connecting all of your creative elements—physical body, energy body, Smart Spot—with the earth, enabling you to bring your ideas into physical reality.

A Grounding Story

Elements in nature are effective visualizations for grounding connections. This story illustrates how a natural part of the earth, a huge boulder, can be visualized to help the person become grounded.

Carolyn Cooke, CEO of Isis for Women, an upscale women's athletic apparel company, describes her concept of grounding:

> My image of grounding is to stand on a rock. Even when the world all around me is having hurricanes or snowstorms, when I'm on my rock I am not involved in any of that. I know I am ungrounded if I find myself lost in the snowstorm with everyone else.
>
> In business I know when I am ungrounded because I feel like I am *inside* the problem. You really cannot make a good decision when all around you, all you can see is what is wrong. You lose your sense of perspective when you are deeply entrenched in the emotion and motivations of others. Getting pulled by these situations will happen whether or not you are grounded, but if you have firmly established your grounding connection you can get back in touch with yourself more quickly and really know what to do.
>
> I make better decisions when I step back from the problem and keep it outside myself. Grounding does this for me.

Benefits of Grounding

The many varied benefits of grounding make you smarter and more creative and allow you to effectively act on your ideas to bring them into reality.

Grounding Makes You Smarter

You are actually "smarter" when you are grounded. Why? Clear thinking is the ability to clearly see core issues in a situation and to quickly and effectively separate what is important from what is not. Complicated situations appear as chaotic jumbles of the essential along with the extraneous. Grounding brings the essential elements into focus. It significantly sharpens the mind's ability to effectively sort wheat from chaff.

How? Your mental "sorting table" works best when there is a place for unimportant issues (the chaff) to go. Grounding is the conduit that allows the unimportant to flow out of you, leaving you free to think faster and more clearly with fewer things to take into account. "Grounding out" the noise means that you can work exclusively with useful information.

Grounding alone, without any other step in the Smart Spot process, can create effective results because it enhances all of your abilities—intelligence, knowledge, planning, analysis, and persuasion. It does this by acting as a lightning rod that sends excess or disruptive energy down to a safe place leaving you clearheaded and free of interference.

A grounded person clearly apprehends the key issue or problem in any situation. He or she is able to separate what is important from the emotions and motivations of others and the myriad details surrounding any complex situation.

Grounding Helps You Focus

Less chaff means less distraction. No more getting sidetracked by little things that loom large when you cannot see the forest for the trees. Grounding enables you to focus on what is important so that you can set realistic goals and enhance intention setting, thus stimulating ideas that are at once innovative and pragmatic.

Focus is critical to any project's success. When you work exclusively with essential factors in any situation you can more easily focus on a workable solution. We will talk much more about focus in Chapter 3, Set an Effective Intention.

Grounding Makes You More Creative

Less distraction means more freedom. Removing the clutter from your thinking process creates enough space for you to clearly see all sides of each grain of essential wheat.

In this way, grounding clears the space for mental "play." Important elements can be combined and reorganized in endlessly innovative ways because there is creative space for them to move around. New patterns develop. Innovative ideas and solutions surface in this expansive place.

This feeling of freedom unleashes creativity. It is in this way that your essential energetic connection, grounding, fuels imagination and inspires ingenuity, and enhances all aspects of intuition. Intuition is the ability to sense your environment with insight. It is also the ability to quickly synthesize huge amounts of information into a meaningful result and to creatively help the solution materialize.

Grounding Makes You More Able to Act on Your Creative Idea

Grounding motivates you to act on your ideas—to bring them into the real world. When you know what is important you are more certain about the creative process. Grounding connects your dreams to the physical plane so that they can be manifested. In Chapter 5 we will discuss acting on your intention in more detail.

Grounding: The Secret to Manifesting on Earth

We have seen that grounding enhances mental sharpness and unleashes creativity by filtering out distractions. Yet it is much more than that.

Grounding is the skill that makes dreams come true. Your grounding connection is the functional intermediary between the dream world of ideas and the concrete physical world.

How does it work? Earth is where the action is. Grounding provides a place for ideas to take root. Ideas can be transformed from visualization to tangible structure something like the way H_2O can be energetically altered into its different states: water, ice, and steam.

Let's take a closer look.

Your body is the vehicle for your creative process. Your mind and abilities are accessed in distinctly different ways when you are in a highly creative state. You may feel creative energy in the upper portion of your body or even sense it in the air around your head.

This exciting condition requires grounding to complete the circuit. You, as creative vehicle, must be connected to both the creative place (above) and the experiential place (below) as shown in figure 3. Your mind is the connection to creative energy. Grounding is your energy connection to the place we *experience* creations—the physical world.

If you think creativity is exhilarating, imagine how exciting it is to develop and then bring a creative idea out into the world with no more intellectual or artistic ability than you have right now! All it requires is learning how to ground—to connect your energy to the earth.

Four Ways to Know When You Are Grounded

You are more grounded when you:

1. Feel confident and in control of your reactions.
2. Feel physically calm and "solid."
3. Feel clearheaded and have mental clarity.
4. Have a sense of your whole body—in particular a feeling that your lower body (your seat, hips, legs, and feet) is in contact and communication with your torso and head.

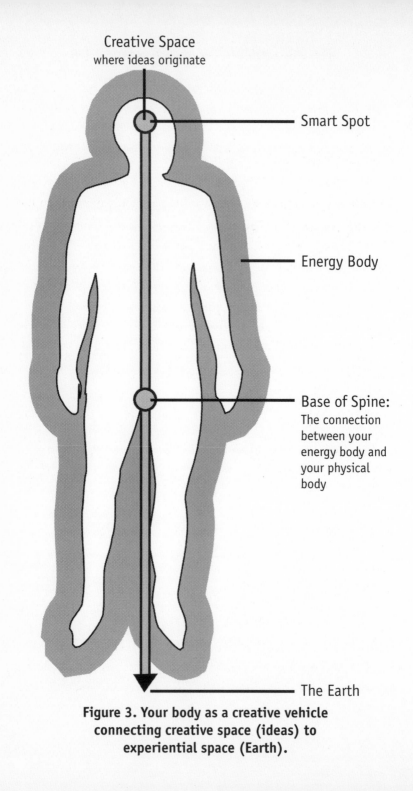

Creative Space
where ideas originate

Smart Spot

Energy Body

Base of Spine:
The connection
between your
energy body and
your physical
body

The Earth

**Figure 3. Your body as a creative vehicle
connecting creative space (ideas) to
experiential space (Earth).**

You are most grounded when all of these things are happening at once. Let's look at each of these ways of experiencing grounding more closely.

Grounding Creates Confidence

Carolyn Cooke's "rock" is her safe harbor. Establishing your grounding connection creates a safe place for you while working in the maelstrom of emotion and panic that are often present in business and other environments. When you do not get pulled in to others' reactions, you can have a more emotionally level demeanor. Being calm allows you to more quickly understand information and to act upon it with confidence and ease.

Grounding Creates Physical Calm

As both Andrew and Carolyn said earlier in this chapter and my students often report, the most immediate benefit they receive from grounding is a state of physical calm. Some people who had previously considered themselves "high strung" or "working best on nervous energy" have discovered that a secure grounding connection helped them use their energy in a more productive way and that they do not tire as easily. Some report that they are no longer exhausted at the end of the workday or week and that they have more interest in and stamina for family, hobbies, and friends.

Grounding Creates Mental Clarity

Perhaps you know the feeling of flying around the room when you get flustered or have too much to do in too little time. That is when you wish someone would scrape you off the ceiling so that you could get something done! If only you could get grounded, connected to the earth, so that you could be productive.

Being airborne is an example of disconnection, of not being firmly in control of your creativity. When grounded, you are better able to see the paths of action that have the greatest likelihood of success. In other words, grounding improves clarity.

A twenty-year veteran of the transportation industry who now consults for the largest retail establishments in the world says it best: "Being grounded gives me the perspective to see the options in any situation and to separate the truth from the lie, the fictional, and the emotional."

So we now know that being grounded is a powerful tool in any decision-making process. That it creates a clear view and calm demeanor. But exactly how does it do this?

The grounding cord (a line of energy that starts at the end of your tailbone and travels down into the center of the earth) gives the commotion, the worry, and extraneous facts somewhere to go! Those things are very disruptive, giving us too much to sift through and think about. And they tend to cloud the issues.

Being grounded is especially important when the situation is complex, has become a crisis, or when other participants are *not* grounded and centered. Providing the voice of reason is good for the company and for your career, whether you are inside the organization or providing a service from the outside.

Grounding Puts You in Touch with Your Physical Body

"Klutzy" days happen when you are not grounded or you are not as grounded as your body requires at that moment. When your entire body is filled with your own energy from your head through your seat, hips, legs, all the way down to your feet, you will actually *feel* different. Many people describe it as "solid," "real," or "ready for anything."

This can make creating anything—even the so-called mundane events in life and work—a smooth, flowing event. It is in these grounded times that my clients and students report that they have a feeling of flow, that they accomplish things more easily than when they are ungrounded.

Getting Grounded

The Role of Awareness

I hope you can see from the above discussion the importance and effectiveness of establishing your grounding connection. Now it is time to learn how to do this for yourself. But to be ready to do this, you need to first build up your awareness. Awareness is the ability to notice behavior and subtle energy feedback in order to expand your perceptive skills.

The first step in learning anything about your energy is to train yourself to notice how things are now, how you would like them to be, and any insights you receive during the process of getting there.

Grounding is about your energy body connecting to and establishing communication with your physical body. You will quickly build your energy vocabulary by starting with what you notice about your physical body. People who do professional "energy work" have an innate ability or have taught themselves to focus directly on energy colors, shapes, and meanings. It is possible that you will not be able to do this right away. That's perfectly OK.

But know this: We are all innately intuitive—it is a fact of being human—and we are all intuitively aware of the state of our bodies, both energy and physical. Why? Because body information is critical to maintaining our health as living organisms. What I am saying is you have everything you need to be intentionally intuitive. *You can do it!*

Bring Your Energy into Your Body

The best way to become aware of your grounding is to take a moment to notice your physical body. How do you feel? Are you agitated? Relaxed? Feeling strong? Do you have a sense that you are floating?

Awareness is about noticing.

Awareness is about focus.

The idea is to pull all of your thoughts from the scattered places they currently reside, back into one location—the inside of your body, the inside of your mind, the inside of your experience at this moment.

Focus your attention on the lower portion of the body—your hips, legs, and feet. Can you feel your feet? Do they hurt? Are they too hot or cold? Does your weight feel evenly distributed along all toes and your heel? How do your ankles feel? Do your legs feel strong or are they tired of sitting or standing too much?

No answer to any of these questions is "right" or "wrong." The important thing is for you to notice what goes on inside your body moment to moment, to sense what happens for you on a subtle level. By noticing, you enhance awareness and ultimately connect consciously to the Smart Spot.

What you are about to do—to become calm, centered, and "smart"—requires giving this much attention to the details of where your awareness is at this moment. As you do the visualization exercises below, continue to be aware of how your body feels.

• •

Visualization 1

Connecting Your Physical Body, Energy Body, and Smart Spot

1. Get comfortable. Find a quiet spot to sit for a few minutes uninterrupted by phones, computers, people, noise, and other distractions. Sit with both feet on the floor, hands in your lap. The goal is to be comfortable and alert.

2. Get calm. Close your eyes. Notice if your mind is filled with analyzing or worry. Visualize mental commotion melting like ice on a warm day. Take as long as you need to remove these mental distractions.

3. Breathe. Breathe in a regular rhythm. Focus on the air as it moves in and then out of your body. Be aware of your body, your feet connected to the floor, your seat connected to the chair. Feel the reassuring heaviness of your body as it sinks into the chair. The goal is to feel quiet inside.

4. Enter the Smart Spot. Become aware of your head— your face, your ears, the back of your head, and the crown of your head. Gather all of your attention at the Smart Spot in the very center of your head and simply notice what is there. Get a "picture" of what this center-of-your-head looks like. Are the lights on or off? Is it expansive and filled with green plants? Is it a seascape? Is it a place that feels comfortable? If not, remodel! Make it a place that feels good to you, a place where you would enjoy spending time. When it feels or looks "right" to you, relax there for a while. Gently pull back any thoughts that stray from this calm, centered awareness.

5. Visualize your energy body. Focus on the space approximately two feet in front of you. Visualize a map or a three-dimensional copy of yourself. This is a "picture" of your energy body. What does it look like? Does it look happy, healthy, complete? Does it have a head, shoulders, arms, torso, legs, and the like? If anything is missing, see if you can gently bring that part into focus. If not, that's fine. Don't force anything. Be excited! You have just had your first look at your energy body!

6. Come in. When you are ready, gently move the map of your energy body three feet above you and slowly bring it down through the top of your head. Move the map

down into your body so that your energy feet are housed within your physical feet; your energy arms within your physical body's arms, and so on.

7. Anchor in. When your physical body is filled with your energy body, you may feel a hum or an increase in vibration. You may hear a tone or simply feel like two aspects of you have come together with a "click." Whatever you see, hear, or sense is perfect. When you are ready, anchor your energy to your physical body at the base of your spine. You may wish to use an actual anchor, a clip, or other attachment. The goal is to be relaxed and aware of your entire body.

8. Welcome yourself "home." Say hello to your self. You've come "home" to your physical body, your energy's true residence on Earth. This beautiful moment is one that many people never experience. If it is an emotional moment for you, that's great. Remain focused on your goal—to notice the sensations in your body and any pictures you "see" or sounds you "hear" as your body communicates with you.

9. Enjoy your space. Take a few minutes to notice how you feel. Do you feel a tingling or warmth? Have you had a change in emotion? Do you feel more "solid" or dense? These are all very good things. Continue to focus on what it is like to have your energy body and physical body in communication with one another. Is this feeling familiar? Enjoy.

Questions to Ask Yourself

- Did you "see" or feel your Smart Spot? Was it comfortable to be there? If not, what did you do to make it more so?

- When you visualized your energy body, was it complete (head, feet, etc.)? If not, what was missing? Were you able to change the picture by bringing attention to the missing part?
- When you moved your energy into your physical body, did you feel a change in sensation? Emotion? Were the feelings familiar? If so, when had you felt them previously?

How to Ground

Now let's add the critical step of grounding to the above visualization.

◦ ◦ ◦ ◦ ◦ ◦ ◦ ◦ ◦ ◦ ◦ ◦ ◦ ◦ ◦ ◦ ◦ ◦ ◦ ◦

Visualization 2

Grounding

Repeat steps 1–7 of Visualization 1 on pages 22–24. Then:

1. Ground. Visualize a line of light from your tailbone connecting you to the center of the earth. Slowly expand this line so that it is as wide as your body. Let go of tension and commotion in your body allowing it to flow through this grounding connection.

    When you feel comfortable with your grounding, sense your feet resting flat on the floor. Visualize a line of energy that connects each foot to the center of the earth.

    You may feel tingling or a slow pulse. Allow gravity to help you down from the ceiling, calm the feeling of flying around the room. Let this reassuring heaviness remind you that you are part of the natural world. Your objective is to feel your body sitting in the chair and to enjoy it!

2. Colorize. Create a protective enclosure about three feet outside of you that completely surrounds your body and the grounding line of energy created in step 1. Choose a color you like or one that comes to you in this quiet space. Fill your enclosure with that color.

3. Notice. Sit without effort in the center of your world.

Note: Your first time grounding will probably take several minutes. With practice you will move easily into this state.

How Deep Is My Grounding?

When you first learn how to ground you may question exactly how deep into the earth your grounding cord should go. In other words, what part of the earth are you connecting to?

Consider this: The top of the earth—the crust—is where volcanoes, tidal waves, high winds, and earthquakes as well as wonderful sunshine, soft breezes, and gentle rain all happen. The core of the earth is wonderfully stable by comparison. That is why we connect all the way to the center of the earth when we ground.

How Do You Know When You Are Grounded?

Physical Feedback

Grounded	Not Grounded
Well-being.	Physically fragile.
Physical vitality.	Feeling spacey, tired.
Sense the health and condition of your physical body.	Feeling "disconnected" from your bottom on the chair, your feet on the floor, and other physical cues.
Sense your connection to the earth.	Disconnection from the physical plane.
Body and energy feel "low to the ground."	Airy, floating. Limited awareness of lower body.
Sense of gravity/feeling solid.	"Not real," not all here.
Moving with ease and grace.	Klutzy/accident-prone.

Emotional Feedback

Grounded	Not Grounded
Calm.	Jittery, nervous, "uptight."
Centered.	Feeling "off-center." Having "one of those days."
"Grounded."	Airy, floating.
Mental clarity.	Fuzzy thinking.
Enhanced awareness.	Reduced ability to notice your body's feelings.
Able to handle anything.	Emotionally fragile.
Feeling of safety.	Insecurity.

Situational Feedback

Grounded	Not Grounded
Synchronicity.	Everything is "off base."
Sense of events being "under control."	Things "happen to" you.
You are observed as competent and reliable.	You are observed as flighty or irrational.
Safety.	Uncertainty.

Physical Enhancements to Grounding

Grounding is your energetic attachment to the physical plane. Situations that are comforting or stimulating to the physical body can enhance your ability to ground. Some examples:

Physical safety
Physical comfort
Security
Love
Nurturing
Food

Exercise
Sufficient and restful sleep
Verbalizing instead of worrying
Doing instead of worrying
Financial security

Ideas Need Grounding, Too

When a person is grounded, he or she has a sense of well-being and creativity. Ideas, plans, and projects must also be connected to the earth's energy field for them to *materialize*. Ideas, too, must be grounded.

Grounding solidifies ideas, making them manifest in the world. Ideas are created "out of thin air." Solutions are often "dreamed." The difference between a blueprint versus a beautiful house on the hill, or a story you made up in your head versus a published book, is the ability to bring the creation out of the clouds and down to earth. The difference is grounding.

A project is grounded when:

1. Things "go like clockwork."
2. Things feel "under control."
3. Creative new ideas and solutions are available at each decision point in the process.

When the idea, dream, or creation is grounded it is often irresistible to participants and may even seem to have wings, allowing it to take off and fly even in the most ominous headwind. Good things happen when they are grounded.

In fact just about any idea will work, no matter how outlandish. Virtually any dream can happen—no matter how remote it may seem at the moment it is conceived—if it is grounded.

Many Ways to Ground a Project

The energetic way to ground projects and ideas is to visualize them in as much detail as possible out in front of you as a movie, a photograph, a painting, or any other visual expression that works for you. Imagine a grounding connection to the bottom of the movie or picture and run it all the way into the center of the earth. Shrink the picture down to six inches or so in height, keep it grounded, and put it in a safe place just outside your energy space. Check on it every once in a while until it is manifested.

You can enhance energy grounding for your idea or project by committing resources to it in the physical world. Here are some examples.

- Proper funding to complete the task creatively and on time.
- Appropriate, motivated, and knowledgeable staff.
- Commitment from upper management.
- Appropriate marketing and sales.
- Adequate number and quality of meetings.
- Validation for jobs well done.
- Incremental (task-by-task) successes.

Grounding is essential to creating anything. All ideas and actions flow from you, that is, your energy body plus your physical body. When your energy is firmly seated in your body and you are grounded to the center of the earth, your creative energy flows easily, enabling you to create virtually anything.

Grounding is the essential first step in the Smart Spot process.

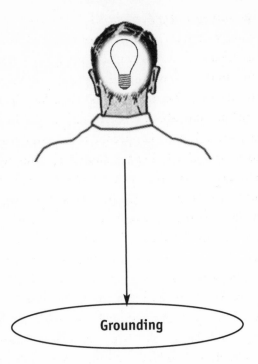

Stories: Grounded Dreams, Ideas, and Plans

Grounded Project #1: "Staying on Intention"

Carolyn Cooke, CEO, Isis for Women:

> Trade shows are the way we introduce new products in the
> outdoor industry. This year the primary outdoor show was
> moved up four weeks because of the Olympics. The only
> date they could move it to was right after New Year's instead
> of January 30th. This meant that it was not going to be
> held at a very good time, but since it was rescheduled for
> a unique reason—the Olympics—I decided that we still
> needed to be represented at this main show.

The skiing trade show, which is in competition with the primary outdoor show but not designed for retailers like Isis, tried to strategically place themselves to have retailers come to their show instead of the less convenient outdoor retailer one. They made a good pitch, but I had already made the decision about representing our products at the primary show. I knew Isis needed to be at the main show and to go to both would have diluted our resources.

Ten days before the ski show was to begin, I was in Anaheim at the primary Outdoor Show. There were many distractions, as there always are at trade events. The ski show representatives did a full-court press on me and other retailers. They made it very attractive by offering free shipping of the booth and other amenities. They kept stressing that there was no time to think about it—just do it.

Amid the chaos at the show I was physically tired and not as grounded as I would like to have been. I nearly said, "Sure, let's do it," but decided on the spur of the moment to take twenty-four hours to make the decision.

Then I stopped, got grounded on the rock, and told myself, "I have already made this decision, and trying to make another decision under duress with just a few moments consideration does not make sense. To change my mind now is a bad business decision."

The next day I told them that although it sounded exciting, Isis was going to stick to its original marketing plan and not go to the ski show.

It turned out to be a great decision. Retailers did not show up as had been promised, so going would have been a lot of wasted effort and eight lost days plus the expense of transporting people and materials to the show.

When I am grounded, I know that there is no decision that needs to be made on the spot!

Energy Explanation

When you are grounded, you know there are almost no decisions in business that need to be made immediately. Second guessing your intentional original decisions while under duress usually means you end up having to fix things later. Grounding and operating from your Smart Spot provide the basis for you to match opportunities with your company's vision—with its intentions. Those types of decisions become very simple. Those that fit, you do. Those that don't, you don't.

Grounded Project #2:
"Grounding Helps You Attract What You Need"

Ann Krcik, Founder and President, Extreme Connection, represents world-renowned adventurers in the corporate arena. She places members of this extraordinary group as motivational speakers and product spokespeople.

Ann's star client was asked to give the keynote speech at a major business conference culminating in a black-tie awards celebration. All of Ann's speakers are dynamic, and this one is a particular crowd favorite, a talented presenter who consistently delivers spellbinding tales to eager corporate audiences.

Used to enthusiastic crowds, both he and Ann were concerned that this event could end up being less successful than normal because his presentation was scheduled on the last day of the conference. Not only was it the last day, but it was at the end of a very long day of meetings and speeches and attendance was optional. Worse still, his speech was the only thing standing between the audience and the much-anticipated black-tie dinner/dance where the industry awards would be given out.

Ann watched with dismay as the day waned and the number of people in attendance at each meeting slid from 500, down to 350, and finally in the event just before the speech, down to less than 100 people.

She decided to ground herself, the room, and the situation and to set up the grounding as an energetic "welcome mat," affirming that the speech would be an inspiring, not-to-be-missed event.

As it turned out, almost all of the conference's 500 attendees came to the speech and the event organizers were thrilled when the speaker went ten minutes over his allotted time because everyone was so enthralled.

Energy Explanation

This story illustrates the wisdom in the phrase "Worry less, ground more." Grounding in and of itself is often all that is required to make any situation more successful. It is by far the most important step in the Smart Spot process.

How did grounding improve this situation? The energy of the conference after several days of meetings and speeches was beginning to get bogged down. As the final, long day of meetings proceeded, participants got tired and unfocused from all of the talking and information. When people get bored, their energy body tends to rise out of the physical body in search of something more creative to focus on. (You wouldn't expect Van Gogh or Einstein to sit in a boring meeting, would you? Your creative energy body also leaves when it gets bored.)

Ann needed to be grounded and operate from her Smart Spot because she was the organizer—the person in charge of the keynote speech. If the leader is ungrounded or not perceiving the situation accurately, it is almost impossible for any event to be on solid footing. Once she was grounded, Ann's creativity was unleashed, and she went into action to energetically ground the meeting hall.

Grounded people, events, and rooms feel solid, worthwhile, and intentional because they are "tuned in" to creative energy while remaining solidly connected to the real world. People nearly always sense a difference when the energy changes in an event, a room, or a location. They know when people's energy changes, too. Grounding is a fundamental statement in the way you appear and "feel" to others.

All of that talk and sitting made the energy at the conference and in the meeting rooms stagnant and boring. When grounded, the auditorium itself began to function as a magnet because it felt good to people—energizing, safe, and attractive.

Grounding the keynote speech communicated to participants that this was not going to be "just another meeting." When the energy around an event is different, people take notice. All of a sudden the creative element within each attendee brightened as if someone had turned on a creative switch.

Participants sensed that the grounded speech was more energized. They could more easily "hear" the message that the speech was going to be a once-in-a-lifetime event and would be a perfect prelude to the evening festivities. That made it easy for them to make the decision to attend.

Grounding is the way to make good things happen and being in the Smart Spot allows you to be aware of when you (or a situation) are grounded or not.

Grounded Project #3:
Grounding Aligns Energy with Intention

Ann was also involved in another story about grounding that all of us can relate to. She was traveling en route to the Bay Area from a major event in which one of her speakers was featured and got stuck in a long line when the airport experienced a breach in security.

Late, tired, and at the end of a line encompassing everyone in the airport (several thousand people), she called to say that the way things were going, she might not be back until the next day. She wanted to become more calm, more physically enlivened, and for things to move along at a faster clip.

Those are key indications that grounding is needed. Whenever things are going haywire, it is a safe bet that the situation is not grounded.

Over the open phone line, we both consciously grounded her *and* her intention (to get home quickly and safely). She admitted that, as much as she wanted to believe that something could be done to help the situation, she was feeling so spent that she didn't have much confidence in the grounding process. Even so, as she focused on her grounding connection and dumped the worry and the exhaustion down the conduit into the earth, she started to feel better. We hung up and I continued to work on grounding her and her intention to get home safely that evening.

Twenty minutes later she called and said, "You won't believe this. They changed the desk where all of the tickets need to be processed and they *switched the line* so that those at the end, including me, are now in front! It looks like I will get home tonight."

I wish I could have taken the credit, but in truth it was her strong intention combined with the effectiveness of grounding that made for a happy and successful ending to the story.

Energy Explanation

Grounding is an essential aspect of intentional intuition. What you need, moment by moment, is always available to you. You can best determine your needs when you operate from the Smart Spot. When your energy is in your physical body and you are grounded, you become an energetic magnet that automatically attracts to you what you need.

How? Energy does not have opinion or judgment. It flows to the most available and "attractive" source—just like water surges most easily downhill and through crevices.

Grounding makes your body a consolidated space that clearly communicates your needs. What you intend automatically flows toward you.

Getting Ready for Step Two

Grounding creates the condition in which good things can happen. Setting an effective intention enhances this process so that only those good things that exactly fit your needs make their way to you.

Read on to learn how.

● *Exercises*

1. Notice the state of your grounding the next time you write a report or letter. Intentionally ground and continue writing. What, if anything, is different?

2. The next time you are in a meeting, sense the state of your grounding. Can you sense the state of grounding for other meeting participants? Is the meeting itself grounded?

● ● ● ● ● ● ● ● ● ● ● ● ● ● ● ● ● ●

Ideas Presented in This Chapter

- The secret to manifesting your creations in the real world (on Earth) is grounding.
- Grounding makes you smarter, helps you focus and be more intentional, makes you more creative and intuitive, and helps you to act on creative ideas.
- Earth is where the action is! Your grounding connection is the functional intermediary between the dream world of ideas and the concrete physical world.
- People *and* projects can be grounded.

Questions to Ask Yourself

- How often am I grounded?
- What situations are easiest for me to be grounded in? Which are the most difficult?
- What physical feedback lets me know when I am grounded?
- What emotional feedback lets me know when I am grounded?
- What situational feedback lets me know when I am grounded?

My Intention for Grounding

Spend a few minutes thinking about how you would like to use the concept of grounding to improve your life or your work. Use the space below to write your intention.

3

S tep Two: Set an Effective Intention

Grounding establishes a solid foundation for the second step in the Smart Spot process—Set an Effective Intention.

An effective intention is a lucid visualization of the goal of any project, meeting, company vision, or lifestyle. By clearly stating the objective, you set a context for creative action. An intention helps everyone and everything involved work toward a common goal.

Robin Toft, CEO, Roy Toft Photography, sets business intentions based upon her experience and imagination:

I [visualize] the outcome that will work best by formulating hypotheses. I read a lot, do some research, and use some intuitive hits and then mull [the intention] over for a while. I usually wake up with a conclusion and then go back and fill in the blanks.

Once set, I already know what is possible—what's going to happen. Then I make a plan so that everyone else can get signed up for it, too.

What Is an Effective Intention?

Intention is a deliberate decision to create. It is premeditated; it is planned. Intention is not a fleeting thought. It is also not a wish, hope, or worry. It is a decision made with purpose to produce something. It is a force unto itself.

An effective intention is a written, verbally stated, or lucid visualization of a desired outcome set in positive terms. It is concise. If written, it is brief and specific, including measurable timing and results. If visualized, it is a complete picture of the desired result in as much three-dimensional detail as you can imagine. Whatever form it takes, the intention is comprehensive and includes all elements essential to a successful result.

Here are some examples of effective business intentions:

- Company vision or mission statements
- Sales budgets and business plans
- New product specifications
- Statement that a product will change the world (along with a description of how it will do this)

Setting an Effective Intention— the Energy Explanation

Setting an effective intention is the shortest route to create virtually anything in your business or your life. Why? A well-envisioned intention collects all aspects of the goal into a compact "arrow" of energy that you aim straight at the target—the objective. Energy is the tool that makes intentions manifest in the world. The more you operate from a place of objective calm—your Smart Spot—and the more you focus your imaginative energy in the right direction and narrow its scope to exactly what is desired, the more creative power you wield to attain the goal.

In the intuitive world this is known as "energy follows thought." What we think, or intend, is what happens.

As you set your intention, keep in mind step 1 of this process: Establish Your Grounding Connection. It is very important to ground everything related to your intention, including inanimate objects such as your project, your business, or your meeting. Grounding the intention is as important as grounding yourself and will significantly improve the chance of success because it gives your idea a place to live and operate in the physical world. Grounding transforms your dream into reality—intentionally!

Benefits of Setting an Effective Intention

Intentions Ground the Creative Process

A comprehensive and strongly held intention grounds the creative process because it concentrates your creative strength directly on the solution or invention. It is the difference between using an energetic shotgun (where the power is sprayed in the general direction of the goal) and an energy rifle, with which power is focused in a narrow trajectory. This concentrated focus distills the energy into a powerful ability to create.

If you are working on a project with other people, intention focuses everyone's creativity on the goal. The result is true creative collaboration. Intention provides precisely what is needed in exactly the right spot at just the right time. No wonder it works.

Intentions Create Specific Outcomes

The more detailed and accurate you are in describing the intention in words or visualizing it in pictures, the greater its chance of coming to fruition as you expect. When visualized in sufficient detail, intention is a filter that effectively sifts out creations that do not match the goal.

I am reminded of a particular sales meeting I attended in my former computer business. The task was to convince a governmental department to engage my firm to provide their data conversion services. Over a period of weeks I introduced my company's products to the key players in the department. When it came time to present the proposal to the department manager, I was warned that he had a volatile personality and never let vendors complete presentations. The technical people (my contacts) were frustrated because they needed a solution and felt strongly that my company had the answer. I agreed.

I remember setting a strong intention for the meeting to be polite and pleasant and for people to enjoy themselves. More than a decade of providing superior quality custom programming had convinced me that once a prospective client heard about our service, they almost always made a decision to go with us. I brought brochures and presentation materials that stated our excellence, but my intention was to make certain that the meeting was polite. It did not focus on the practical aspects of presenting my firm's service or directly answering client needs. I had spent twelve long years seriously building the firm's reputation for customer-indulgent service and superior-quality work. I assumed that these facts were self-evident.

The upshot was that the meeting was very polite, but you may not be surprised to learn that my firm was not awarded the contract. It went to the company with the "serious" representative.

From then on, I used the method that had worked for more than a decade—focusing intentions through the prism of the excellence of our work and overlaying the more subtle aspects, no matter what personalities were involved. Sticking to my original formula was what I found to be repeatedly successful.

Intentions Quickly Create What You Want

An intention is not just a mental goal—it is an idea that has been elevated to a "thoughtform" through your energetic creative process. As your idea is transformed from a mere thought originating in your Smart Spot to an external, grounded intention, it becomes a physical structure in the world. With practice, your visualizations can become so well defined and grounded that activities and goals begin happening the moment you think them.

During a recent transition in my life, I started to play music from another creative time decades earlier. I put away my favorite classical and jazz CDs and became addicted to old-time rock 'n' roll—especially the song "Kathmandu" by Bob Seger and the Silver Bullet Band. If you've heard it, you may agree that the song is loud and compelling—an energetic force unto itself.

I knew that times of transition can challenge one's grounding, so I worked constantly on that as the events of my life shifted around me. I drove around town doing mundane things while listening to the song at full volume. It helped me not to worry so much and created a buoyant, happier feeling. I played it over and over again—perhaps one hundred times in a two-week period. It never ceased to please me.

In the song, Seger loudly asserts again and again that if he ever gets out of here, he's going to Kathmandu! At that point in my life I wanted nothing more than to escape old, constricting boundaries. I *did* want to get out of the situation and out of town, and my energy body took this repeated message literally and set about creating an exotic trip.

A few days later a woman I had met only twice in professional situations and who has since become a close friend brought up the idea of travel to Nepal. At that time I rarely journeyed abroad and was especially naïve about third-world Asia.

Playing the song "Kathmandu" over and over again created a clear intention. There was no ambiguity. My energy body received the message loud and clear: I wanted to go to Kathmandu (not just "any exotic land" or "an Asian country") and I wanted it *now*.

Within weeks, the intention "Kathmandu—now!" was made manifest as I sat in a bazaar in Kathmandu, Nepal, making final preparations to trek the Himalayas for a full month. Imagine! Me! Someone who had never considered going to Asia and certainly not the third world, had never camped before, and even had to purchase her very first hiking boots for this trip.

Me at Mount Everest! Quite an intention.

It is instructive to note that I did not set an intention for, nor even think much about, the physical aspects of the trip. I did not have a burning desire to hike for ten-plus miles per day; to live for a month without heat, electricity, or running water; or even to visit the awe-inspiring site of Mount Everest.

Yet the "exact match" of Kathmandu and the timeframe of "now" was precisely met by going on the trip. My general interest in matters of human enlightenment and the world of subtle energy created a context for the intention because the Himalayas, which extend into Tibet, are a very energetically active place. The "wild cards" of trekking and camping were not in opposition to the intention of "Kathmandu—now!" even though I did not specifically visualize them.

Perhaps you have heard the expression, "Be careful what you wish for; you might get it." The more you visualize or "hear" as many aspects of your intention as possible—really flesh it out with inspiring detail—the more you can be assured that you are creating exactly what you want.

This idea gives new meaning to the importance of the screen-saver picture on your computer, photos or illustrations on desk calendars, photos or other objects on your desk, the music you enjoy most, and the thoughts that occupy your daydreams. It is very possible that you are setting effective intentions with every one of these aspects of your normal work and personal life.

Is that what you intend?

At the time I went to Asia my life was opening to new possibilities and in truth I probably could not have used a logical thinking process to plan a trip so unusual and life-changing.

My trip to Nepal was an only-to-be-dreamed event made even more special by the fact that it was created with a song.

Qualities of Effective Intentions

Intentions Set Measurable Objectives

How will you know if your intention worked? The easiest way is to set it up with its own measurement for success. Instead of intending a project to be "lucrative," visualize a minimum, specific dollar figure—either gross or net—and make that an integral part of the intention. You might consider leaving the upper end open because creative action can turn into an undreamed-of success. When the project is completed and you are paid, you will know if your intention was barely effective or wildly so.

Intentions Must Be Grounded to Be Effective

Bringing an idea "down to earth"—visualizing it and then making it manifest here on the planet—requires grounding. All of the significant benefits of being grounded as a person apply to grounded intentions. Grounded intentions are more effective, less prone to others' whims and invalidation, and much more easily implemented than those that are ungrounded.

Ungrounded intentions are not really intentions at all. They are wishes or dreams wafting about on thin air. Once connected to the earth, intentions can be manifested in a physical, active way.

Intentions Must Have Energy Integrity

Intentions work best when they are in energy integrity. What does this mean? I assume that you do not intentionally wish to hurt someone or cause harm, but there are times when desiring a certain outcome will interfere with others' free will—with their choice to operate as they wish in the world. Controlling others is not in energy integrity.

The easiest way to ensure alignment with the concept of integrity is to set your intention to achieve the "highest outcome for all." The specific details of your goal will be guided by this important statement of intention.

Two Types of Intentions

There are two main types of intuitive goals: "everyday" intentions, and "grand" intentions.

Everyday intentions are "regular life" goals—those that fill our days such as getting to work on time, finishing a project already in motion, or picking up the kids after school.

In business, everyday intentions include making sure a one-hour meeting stays within a sixty-minute timeframe, choosing an appropriate sales manager based upon a specific set of predefined skills and personality traits, getting a good parking space, and operating within a budget.

Grand intentions are similar in that they set goals; the goals are simply much bigger. In fact, grand intentions relate to life purpose—the reason you are on the planet at this time and exactly what you are uniquely qualified to accomplish.

Grand intentions apply to business, too. They relate to the "life purpose" of an organization or an industry. They can be big transformations like a change in corporate culture. Other grand intentions in business might be changes in paradigm, such as significantly increasing or decreasing the size of a firm, going global, or changing a company's name, identity, or heartland business.

As we saw in Chapter 1, a grand business intention was set by Apple Computer in the 1980s. Their goal was to change the world by providing easy, wide access to the world of information. And it has happened.

Everyday Intentions

On the surface, deciding what you want in the normal events of life seems fairly easy. Let's take a closer look.

When you get into your car in the morning to go to work or take the kids to school, you have a baseline expectation that you will not be in an accident or that road construction or some other obstruction will not delay your arrival. Therefore your intention is to arrive safely and on time. We set many of these everyday intentions throughout our day.

Let's say you get up in the morning and think, "I sure hope there is no problem on the freeway this morning. I don't like arriving late to work." By thinking this thought, you have already begun a process of intention. Worry intentions are just as powerful as positive ones and when you visualize a worry situation in detail, you ground it, making it very powerful indeed. Because "energy follows thought," your worry thought changes the smooth energy pattern between your home and your office.

If you erase that thought with the positively stated intention, "I will arrive at work safely and on time," and visualize the details of this fact, you stand a much better chance of arriving safely and on time.

Another way that progress can be muddled is if someone else sets an intention *for* you. Let's say your spouse wants to talk about vacation plans and you were too tired the previous evening to finish the conversation. Your significant other's expectation is that you will continue the discussion in the morning because "there are some things that are more important than arriving on time to work."

Your spouse's intention is that you will *not* necessarily arrive at work on time—that is, if you do not first finish talking about vacation plans.

If you do not set an intention and someone else (in this case, your mate) sets an effective one, guess what's likely to happen? In this example, you might arrive safely to work, but you probably will not arrive on time.

There are two possible ways that an intention can be diverted. One is through worry thinking and the second is through an incrementally stronger intention being set by another person.

Attitude also sets intention. For instance, you may not have that vacation discussion if you are strongly opposed to it. Strong emotion can create a superseding intention. Let's say you want to defer the conversation until you have had a chance to research airfares to each of the proposed destinations. In that case, instead of having the vacation conversation, you might have an argument about leaving in the middle of an important discussion (your mate's perception) when you should have left for work ten minutes ago (your side of the story).

There are other influences that might make you late (or compromise your safety, for that matter). If you knew, for instance, that there was a pileup on the freeway just one mile from your office that morning, you could change the route you use to get to work. This type of information can be available to you through the enhanced perception of your Smart Spot. In Chapter 4, Access Your Creative Intuition, we will explore the possibilities of pre-seeing a situation so that you can set a more effective intention.

In short, being grounded and setting an effective intention each morning sets the tone for your day and greatly improves synchronicity and your effectiveness. These two acts align you with your creative energy and ground it for manifestation. You have also set an intentional target toward which creative ideas and solutions can be directed. Being grounded and intentional removes your fate from the whims of the gods and puts it squarely in your own court.

Grand Intentions for Business

A grand intention is basically a life purpose—the person or organization's reason to exist. You might think this to be a totally different question, requiring a process poles apart from everyday-intention setting. Nothing could be further from the truth. Every intention, grand or everyday, is set by knowing what you want to create, grounding it, and clearly stating it as powerfully, as specifically, and as often as necessary to achieve the goal.

A good example of this phenomenon is PGP Corporation. This firm was foundering under governmental regulations and unclear intentions until four men joined ranks to buy the company. Their overall intention? To create a software security product that would be so important to the computer industry and to individuals that it would be adopted nearly unanimously all over the world.

Within a scant few months, they formed the idea and approached several companies for venture capital funding, struck a workable deal to buy the company, built a management team, hired staff, located office space, redesigned the logo, and created a new website with commerce capability. They also planned a new product launch.

It worked with some industry fanfare. The new owners had to create all manner of grand and everyday effective intentions—one after the other—setting and resetting goals as the new company moved through the developmental process.

This company was created in an astoundingly short period of time, proving that with single-minded focus, creative collaboration, and intention anything is possible.

An Intentional Story

A very effective way to set an intention is to build your goal around the lifestyle you desire. The details—a future career, formalization of a relationship, or even an important hobby that turns into one's life work and more can all happen in response to an overview intention set with absolute conviction.

The following story told by writer and editor Cheryl Kimball illustrates how she and her partner set a series of effective intentions to create their dream lifestyle. Commitment to an overriding grand intention is a great way to direct all of the individual decisions—the everyday intentions—as circumstances change over time. Each of these ancillary intentions was consistent in support of the original lifestyle objective. In Cheryl's words, "We know that we have the life we have because we wanted it and we created it. I guess you would say we set an intention."

I certainly would!

Cheryl Kimball tells her lifestyle intention tale:

I think the real intention I set way back was to live a certain lifestyle. There were several steps along the way to get to where I am now.

In the spring of 1990, I took a position as an associate production editor with a book publisher in my town. Over the course of six and a half years, I ended up as publisher of their $2 million trade book division, a career move that put me on the management team of a company owned by the then-third-largest publisher in the world.

I spent a year focusing on my new job, but by the spring of '91 I was looking for something "physical" to do. I had ridden horses in my teens and had a horse for a couple of years in my early twenties, so I decided to take some lessons. I enjoyed them, then bought a horse from a friend.

The horse was the catalyst for my becoming involved in the pursuit of good horsemanship. In my search to figure out how to deal with this two-year-old powerful animal who hadn't yet been ridden, I discovered a group of people who looked at training horses differently from how I had been taught. Suddenly the horse became a project that led me to a way of thinking. My intention here was that I wanted to do things differently, and so I set out to find a way. If I hadn't been open to it, the great horsemanship teachers that I found wouldn't have appeared or I wouldn't have recognized them.

The horse also became the impetus for a new lifestyle. My partner and I decided we would like to move from our city townhouse to the country, and we began to look around for a property.

We finally found our place to buy in the fall of 1993—an early 1800s house with three-story barn, carriage house, pond, miles of stone walls, and ninety acres of land. We moved in, now with two dogs, in December, and by summer, my horse and a new filly I had been given, came home.

Just as our lifestyle was beginning to take shape, Jack's company closed its New Hampshire office. Rather than accepting a transfer to the Chicago office, Jack found his dream job in Wisconsin and decided to take it.

In May of 1995, after only fifteen months in our dream home, he left the yard with a U-Haul in tow and moved to Wisconsin. I opted to stay at our farmhouse at least until he decided if he was going to stick with the job. As he left, we set an intention for him to quit and come home if this situation came to seriously jeopardize our relationship.

I was miserable for the next four years, not my intention at all! I stayed in the East for almost two years, then moved to the Midwest with Jack. Our new intention? Under all circumstances, we were keeping our farm in New Hampshire. I took a job as publishing director of a medium-sized company.

For two years Jack and I made more money than we ever had. We rented a twenty-one-acre farm in Wisconsin, and I brought one of my horses with me. We were also able to keep our place in New Hampshire without renting it to anyone. My intention for keeping the house unoccupied was so that I could return home at a moment's notice.

By January of my second year in the Midwest, I made a clear intention to head home by spring. I started gathering together some money and organizing things at the company so that my second-in-command could easily take over as publishing director. In April, as intended, I headed back east with my dog, my horse, and my computer. Jack started making his plans to return. By August, he quit his job and came home to join us in New Hampshire. I was in heaven.

Our general intention was to live and work on the farm, write books and articles, and start a small publishing company. Our specific intention for ourselves, however, was simply to be in control of our own time. What are we doing now? Living and working on the farm, writing books, and building a small publishing company. We are living our intention—we are both in control of our own time. I ride my horses almost every day, we are often land-rich and cash-poor, and most times we are so content we can hardly believe it ourselves.

I did not set out with an intention of having a life that revolves around horses, but along the way, I became so intrigued by the quest for good horsemanship, that I used my writing to explore it. Then I began to realize that, having started three and soon four horses of my own under saddle, I had a bit of experience. So it was a natural offshoot, and I am now working on my third and contracting my fourth book about horses.

After eighteen years together, Jack and I recently got married. Our latest intention: not to let marriage change anything about our good relationship. So far that has worked.

Do we think we are lucky to be living our hoped-for lifestyle? Yes, I do think luck is involved, but we know that we have the life we have because we wanted it and we created it. I guess you would say we set an intention.

Cheryl and Jack set effective intention after intention in their quest to create their lifestyle. The process they used is different from the way most people create their lives. They intentionally decided what they wanted and then made considered decisions every step of the way based upon that intention. Their intentional approach has been spectacularly effective over the long term.

Everyone can create such a life based on long-held dreams. Read on to find out how.

How to Set an Effective Intention

You have just read some stories about effective intention setting—both grand and everyday. Are you ready to learn how to enact and commandeer the great creative energy that is your birthright? Are you ready to learn the simple yet powerful process of setting an effective intention?

In Chapter 2 we discovered that establishing your grounding connection is the first essential step in the Smart Spot process. Step 2 is setting an effective intention. It starts with knowing what you want.

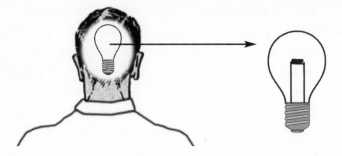

An idea is born

Knowing What You Want to Create

Knowing what you want to create or solve is part of an internal brainstorming process in which you explore your or your organization's needs. It requires knowing what you *want,* not just what you *don't want,* and then believing that you (or the organization) deserve the desired thing or situation.

The Smart Spot process requires that you have a very clear idea of the desired outcome. It also requires "seeing" it in your mind's eye, stating what you want in clear terms, creating energetic enthusiasm for it, and ultimately recognizing and embracing it when it arrives.

When "what you want" is very straightforward, the intention-setting process is easily within reach, taking what you already know you want from the idea stage to manifestation. However, sometimes knowing what you want can be the hardest part of creating it.

Will You Recognize It When It Says "Hello"?

I cannot imagine anything more important in the creative process than learning to recognize "it"—the desired situation, person, place, or thing—when it arrives and accepting it with enthusiasm and action.

I have several friends who instantly recognized their life partner when they first met, not in the way you may think. They first "knew" the person by how turned off they were by him or her! They have often said that they "couldn't stand" the person until they were "forced" to work together or be together or kept running into each other, and finally had to sit down and admit that they were perfect for each other.

On the other hand, I also know two lucky couples who had exactly the opposite reaction—they instantly recognized their partners as such upon first meeting.

It is faster and easier to instantly recognize what you want when it arrives, but even if it takes a little work to get there, embrace it with the joy of having accomplished a major achievement. Because it is!

When You Don't Know What You Want

What if you don't know what you want to create either for yourself or your organization? What you want may be obscured by there being no obvious good choices, or it could be that there are too many options. Perhaps the question itself is so enormous that you want to give up even before you begin to think about solving it.

These situations often involve a change in life purpose or shift in paradigm or whenever there is inherent ambiguity in the outcome. At times like these, how can you or your organization possibly "know what you want"?

You might start with something that you do *not* like about your current life—your job, your relationship, some aspect of your physical appearance, or anything else—big or small. Then, decide how you want to *experience* the result—in other words, decide how you want to *feel* about it. Let's use an internal brainstorming process to explore a personal life example—a desire to change career.

Brainstorm

Deciding How You Want to Feel

Changing jobs without knowing which industry or type of position would interest you can be overwhelming to think about—all those things that will need to happen to achieve a good result! Even just deciding which area of the world, which country, which state, which city you wish to work in is a big task. You also need to decide the type of position you want and ultimately the company you want to work for at a particular salary with a stated set of benefits. You might even want to start your own business. On its face, this is an enormous undertaking! No wonder there are so many books and classes available on this topic.

Consider trying a different method. Instead of viewing it as a problem, approach the situation as an opportunity to *create* something new. Begin with how you want to *feel* about the outcome. Notice how positioning the question for a creative result instantly moves the frame surrounding the picture. The center of the visualization has changed, and you immediately begin to focus on the exciting, new aspects as opposed to future possible problems. This is a very creative energetic condition.

How do you want to *feel* when you are doing your job? How do you want to feel about yourself when you talk about your job? How do you want to feel about the accomplishments you achieve through your work? Think about how you will feel about the people you will come into contact with—vendors, clients or customers, employees, management. And think about how those types of people make you feel about yourself and your abilities.

Attributions such as "valuable," "intelligent," "having fun," "working in alignment with my highest purpose," "entertained and entertaining," "inspiring to others and myself," are all valid but they are just the beginning. There are thousands of descriptions about ways to feel useful, excited, happy, significant, renewed, and content.

Consider writing down each description that occurs to you so that you collect a series of building blocks for your intention. Know that these are the ideas presenting themselves to you at this point in your life. They could change, but the ways you want to feel are often with you during your whole life.

If this process works for you, the written steps will later remind you of your creative process. If it seems like a very long time since anyone has asked you how you feel about anything, you might consider asking yourself more often.

What Gives You the Feeling You Want?

Armed with your written attribution list, start to notice what situations, which people, and what types of interactions create the feelings you want to have. You can do this by being aware—while doing your current work, eating in a restaurant, interacting with others, or enjoying leisure time. Your intuitive mind will amplify and connect with ideas in other aspects of your life.

Try not to focus on "The Answer to the Problem" of figuring out your new career. Set aside the need to "work" on a specific job description or area of professional expertise. Remember that you are trying to get at what makes you happy and interested—how you want to *feel* about your work, a project, your business or clients, and so on.

Do you love to constantly learn new things? Do you enjoy being a "ham" in front of an audience? Do you like helping people? How? Emotionally? Physically? Intellectually? Do you prefer to work with men? Women? Children? Smart people? Eccentric folks?

Does it make you feel "on your purpose" if you work in solitude? Or do you prefer collaborating on projects, sharing ideas, and testing your abilities in challenging situations?

Do you like a peaceful and quiet environment, or does visual, auditory, or other stimulation make you thrive?

Ask yourself an essential question: *"What makes me smile?"* Do you grin when you see others developing their skills? Are you happiest when you are constantly busy, in the flow? Do you prefer to work alone or do you like a busy, people-filled ambience?

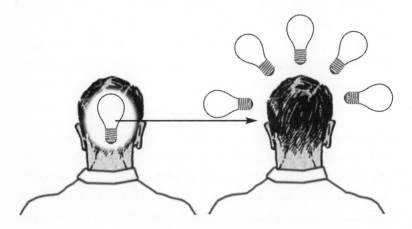

Select an option

Another indication of harmony with one's work is the concept of "flow." In *Flow: The Psychology of Optimal Experience*, Mihaly Csikszentmihalyi's treatise on the pleasure derived from focused activity, the author explains that time passes very quickly when you are fully engaged intellectually, emotionally, and energetically, even if the activity is not what most people would traditionally consider to be "pleasant."

One compelling example is that of mountain climbing. Csikszentmihalyi explains that the rock climber is so focused on not making a misstep (and therefore endangering his life), that he loses all track of time. Or as humorously observed in *Surely You're Joking, Mr. Feynman!* by Nobel Prize–winning physicist Richard Feynman: Ten minutes spent kissing a pretty girl feels much shorter than ten minutes sitting on a hot stove.

Take notice of which activities keep you "in the flow." What consistently makes you lose track of time? Talking on the phone? Surfing the Internet? Mixing different colors of paint? Writing a short story?

If you notice what makes you happiest as you go through your days—workdays, leisure days, weekends, vacation time—you will discover significant pieces of the puzzle to "what you want."

I suggest that you write it all down—no matter how unimportant a small insight might appear to be. Every one is a clue to deciding what you want.

Visualize Perfection

Now that you know how you want to feel, and who and what makes you feel that way, visualize a situation that provides *all* of the attributes you have written down. It doesn't have to be a situation that you know is common enough to be attainable. If your idea of "perfect" is being a medical healer in an office that only serves women between the hours of 9 A.M. and 2 P.M. three days per week and that gives you time to golf and to write that novel you have been putting off, then write that down. Every aspect of it.

Be as specific as possible and as outlandish as necessary to meet every one of your desired feelings. Leave nothing out.

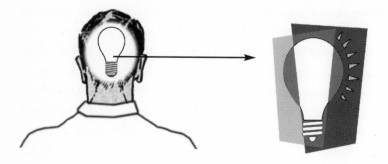

Visualize the details

In the twenty-first century we have more options than ever before. Brainstorming is the time to *expand* your possibilities. Other people and life itself can effectively tackle the very best plans. If you limit yourself at this point in the process before anyone or any thing has had a chance to take you down a notch, then you are already working against your creative intention.

I challenge you to go for everything you want! Why? *Because you can have it.* What you want truly is within your grasp.

Do You Really Deserve It?

It is great that you have figured out what you want. Now, before you create it, is the time to prepare yourself to enthusiastically accept the desired thing or situation when it arrives. This is a very creative moment. Like a jigsaw puzzle, a uniquely shaped energy space opens up to exactly accommodate your desire—every aspect of it, down to the smallest detail.

The amount of time that this special space exists changes as does everything in the world from moment to moment. If you have prepared well and present your precisely constructed intention at exactly the right moment, the "magic" of creation happens.

It's like a theatrical performance. The actors have spent months learning their lines and how to move their bodies to get across to the audience the feeling the character possesses at that moment. The musicians have learned all of the notes and nuances of all of the pieces of music that will be played that evening. The costumes were meticulously designed and sewn, and all of the details—jewelry, shoes, the pipe the father is smoking—every detail is appropriate and right on the mark. The lighting manager has read the script many times and knows exactly when to create a rosy glow or a brilliant spotlight.

The set is perfect—every tree, every piece of furniture, the fog rolling in from the hills in the morning, the moon glowing softly through the windows at night.

Many nights the performance is very good. Everything happens as it is supposed to right on cue. And yet there are a very few nights when magic occurs. The lights, the music, the scenery, and the acting all come together to create something that has never happened before. It is a unique occurrence, and those who are in the audience and on stage and in the orchestra pit that night all know it.

It is that very thing—a flash of magic—that describes the moment of creation. If you are willing to do whatever it takes to discover what you really want, and if you know you deserve it and will accept it when it arrives, you create a thrilling space of time in which the intention is fulfilled.

The following visualization may help you to achieve the feeling that you deserve what you want.

● *Try this:*

See yourself sitting in that new car, or next to your ideal
mate, or in full creative expression in your new career.
How do you look sitting there in your desired situation?
Do you look comfortable? Do you know what to say?
How to act? Do you need a haircut?

● ● ● ● ● ● ● ● ● ● ● ● ● ● ● ● ● ● ● ●

One important way to get what you want is to look the part or
"act as if" it is already happening. So take that dance class, get
your hair highlighted (or cut or curled), learn French (or Spanish or
Russian), and, most of all, figure out what you need in order to
feel like you *deserve* that which you desire.

If it is a new job, find out as much as you can about the culture
and objectives of the organization, and if you still want it after this
discovery, if it still fits your needs and plans for yourself, then imagine how your unique and special persona will complement the needs
and goals of the organization.

Still need a haircut (or a class or some therapy)? Excellent. It
gives you a concrete set of goals to work toward, and the fulfill-
ment of dreams is greatly facilitated by any action taken toward a
goal. It creates an energetic momentum that is at once subtle and
very powerful. We will talk much more about momentum in Chapter 5, Act with Intention.

In the meantime, know that by *not* taking that class or getting
that haircut you are *also* acting. It is action not likely to achieve
the dreamed-of result.

Intention is a deliberate decision to create something. When
you can genuinely see yourself in the new situation, you have made
an important decision. That choice is based on knowing that you

deserve what you want because you can visualize it in detail and are ready for it to happen.

The Creative Act of Visualization

To create what you really need and want in your life you must visualize the desired thing or situation. The more specific your visualization, the more successful the outcome is likely to be.

What makes a visualization "specific"? See if you can come up with an aspect of the purpose that you can taste. Is it salty? Sweet? Sour? Does the taste linger on the tongue? Is there an aroma associated with it? Is it pleasant? Or not?

See the colors, the texture, the participants, what they are wearing, the appearance of the room, the organization (or chaos), and anything else that appears to be significant. Don't forget the details—the more, the better. It will help you to genuinely "be there" and that is very creative.

Are there other people involved in your intention? What are they saying? Do their voices sound happy? Excited? Interested? Bored? Is there music? If not, should there be? Do you hear a sound that sets the "tone" for the event?

How does the situation feel? Is it hot or cold? Sharp? Soft? Happy? Provocative? Complex?

If you are working on a new relationship, how do you want to feel about that connection? Joyful? Enthusiastic? Comfortable? Validated? Beautiful? Intelligent? Adored?

If it is a project, how would you describe the desired outcome? $20,000 of profit? Everyone involved is excited about working together again soon? Do you want to learn some important new skill or process? Do you want the project to lead to further work or generate new business contacts throughout the industry or vertical market?

The important thing is to make the desired outcome as tangible as possible and then visualize that tangibility. See it, feel it, and if appropriate or possible, taste it and hear it. Sense all aspects of the goal. The more "real" it is to you—the more three-dimensional the picture, the more vivid the sensations—the closer you have brought the idea to reality. Visualizing in this way actually begins to ground the intention even before it goes to the next step. A well-envisioned and grounded intention is the shortest route to manifesting anything on Earth.

Knowing what you want and possessing a sense of entitlement—knowing that you deserve the desired thing—and seeing, feeling, sensing the details have prepared you to create an effective intention, a very clear message that you know what you want and that you are ready for it to happen.

Stop for a Minute—Assess Your Goal

Once you have the picture of what you want to create visualized in specific detail, let the visualization sit with you for a few minutes, hours, or days. The timeframe will depend upon the importance and complexity of the intention. If it is a lifestyle intention—one that will affect every aspect of how you experience the rest of your life—you will probably want to give it more than a few moments' consideration. If it is about selecting the best outfit for a cocktail party, you might be able to do that in just a few minutes.

Why wait at all? Because the intention you set is going to be so effective that you *will* create it. Therefore, it is important to visualize as accurate a picture as possible of what you *really* want. If that takes a few extra minutes or days, or requires consulting with your significant other or the management team, then that time may well be worth the brief delay.

Six Ways to Set an Effective Intention

The Integrity Intention

The fastest and easiest way to ensure that your own actions and those of your organization are ethical is to create an integrity intention. You may wish to add integrity wording to every intention you set in business and in any situation in which you collaborate or depend upon the actions of others. It will act as a filter and set the standard through which all activity—intentional and not—is measured and decided upon.

The words of the integrity intention are simple: "Highest outcome for all." It speaks volumes in the subtle energy world.

Energy Explanation for the Integrity Intention

Being in energetic integrity means that you and your organization are not imposing your will upon others. It means that people and other groups are free to decide and act as they wish without control from you or your business.

This is a very big concept and an entire book could be written about the subject. Suffice for now to say that in the current climate of terrorist activities and unethical business practices, it is never too soon or too frequent to clearly state an intention for organizational integrity. When you and everyone else in the organization direct some of your creative energy toward the intention for an outcome that is the highest for all concerned, you have aligned yourself with the ethical, creative power of the universe.

The Business Vision Statement Intention

The vision statement is a business's most significant intention. It states the reason the company exists and clearly communicates how it operates ethically in the world. A clear vision statement is the filter through which all energy in and around the organization flows. It is a clear, unambiguous statement of business philosophy and sets forth in as few words as possible exactly what people both inside and outside can expect when interfacing with your organization.

In their book, *Leaders: The Strategies of Taking Charge,* Warren G. Bennis and Burt Nanus, two of the classic writers on leadership, describe how vision functions:

> To choose a direction, a leader must first have developed a mental image of a possible and desirable future state of the organization. This image, which we call a *vision,* may be as vague as a dream or as precise as a goal or mission statement. The critical point is that a vision articulates a view of a realistic, credible, attractive future for the organization, a condition that is better in some important ways than what now exists.

The vision must be something that all people involved can support. Howard D. Mehninger in *School Reform in the Information Age* noted that vision is a "mental image of a desirable state of affairs. By setting direction, a vision statement helps set priorities and guides policy."

This vision is then translated into a vision statement that, according to Mehninger, should:

- Describe a desirable future that would be better than the present or the past,
- Be achievable in a reasonable amount of time, and
- Take advantage of opportunities the future will afford.

A well-crafted vision statement reflects your organization's ethics and values. It also communicates the group's intentional process to interface with the outside world—customers, vendors, business partners, the community, and the country or world at large.

To serve its function as inspiring force, a vision statement must be clear, engaging, and attainable. To be motivating, it must touch deep values and hopes.

● *Try this:*

1. Ground and center yourself. This is in preparation to do something very important—visualize your organization's future.

2. Set an effective intention for your organization by writing a vision statement that includes the following:

   • Reason the business or organization exists (what you intend to accomplish)

   • Product or service

   • Statement of ethical philosophy

3. Set it aside for a day or two, then reread it to see if it communicates everything you want to say. Revise as necessary.

4. Ask two of the most intuitive people you know whose business acumen you trust to review your vision statement. Ask them what they think it means. Consider revising the statement if the reply indicates reader confusion.

5. Revise as necessary.

● ● ● ● ● ● ● ● ● ● ● ● ● ● ● ● ● ● ● ●

Energy Explanation for the Vision Statement Intention

The words of its vision statement are an articulation of a business's most powerful intention. It sets direction and in this way helps set priorities and guide policy. The vision statement *sets the energy* around everything that happens in your organization. It is the cornerstone of every word, every service, every product, every proposal, and every invoice that is created by or emitted from your business. It does this because it is a vivid visualization—a filter through which all activities and goals are decided and implemented.

The Five-Minute "Set Your Day for Success" Intention

The human resources vice president for a technology company, one of my clients, understood what made people love their jobs (or hate them) and became quite good at interviewing and selecting successful employees. David came to me for an intuitive consultation to help him decide if he should start his own executive search firm. He was about to get married and had just bought a huge new house in northern California so he was understandably concerned about cash flow.

I could see that he had a lot of information about the service that he wanted to provide, but in the consultation I sensed something even more critical: he had an innate ability to set very effective intentions. There were many times that he had simply "decided" to do something—stop smoking, scale mountains, and accurately select appropriate individuals for specific positions in the company—and it happened almost instantaneously. He did not understand the phenomenon, but he did know that it worked and depended upon it in both his personal life and in business.

There was little question that he would meet with success with his new venture, but the speed with which this would happen was tied to his ability to focus on his goals and create immediate demand for his new "headhunter" service.

He asked me for a technique that he could learn during the course of the consultation and use every day to help ensure success. For the rest of the hour we discussed (and he practiced) setting an effective intention.

David creatively distilled the process down to the essentials and was able to focus the energy of each entire workday into five minutes of specific intention setting. The key to his success is good advice for us all:

1. Make your intentions as specific as possible, for example, "By the end of this day I will have successfully signed two new clients for our Business Basics Software Package."
2. Believe in them absolutely; in other words refrain from sabotaging your intention.

David was instantly successful with this technique. His willingness to be specific in setting intentions and to focus his daily thoughts and activities in a positive way around those goals has created enormous success.

Soon after starting his business he was able to create in six months the amount of new business he needed for the entire following year. This success has continued.

It is easy to create a Five-Minute "Set Your Day for Success" intention.

● *Try this:*

1. Set up with the grounding visualization on page 25.
2. List up to three things you want to accomplish that day. State each as follows, "By the end of this day I will have successfully completed _____."
3. Go through your day with these thoughts "in mind."

● ● ● ● ● ● ● ● ● ● ● ● ● ● ● ● ● ● ● ●

Energy Explanation for the Five-Minute "Set Your Day for Success" Intention

The reason this type of intention works well is because it is so simple. There is virtually no time to get into all of the back-and-forth dialogue inside your brain that can create negative thinking and processing. When you quickly state the goal, you "view" it without the distraction of all of the reasons that it cannot or will not work. With intense focus (in other words, by eliminating distraction), the intention is automatically grounded and simply and effectively happens.

With practice, you will receive confirmation that your intentions start being implemented the moment you "think" about them. In other words, energy immediately follows your thoughts. What you intend happens.

The "Walk-Through" Intention

John Walsh, chancellor of Greenwich University, Australia, gives an example of a Walk-Through intention. John was a participant in one of my workshops on "Energetic Meeting Management." He explained that when he was a practicing barrister (lawyer), he was accustomed to arriving at the courthouse one hour before court convened. He spent the hour walking through the courtroom touching every chair, standing in front of the judge's stand and the witness stand, and sitting in and familiarizing himself with the feeling of the room.

During the workshop every participant experienced perceiving and changing the energy setting in a meeting room. Afterward, John said that he now understood that he had actually been setting the energy by walking through the room and setting an intention by previewing all of the events that might happen during the court session.

This is similar to the walk-through visualizations that Olympic athletes do before an important meet or contest. It has been pragmatically confirmed that athletes in tennis, baseball, basketball, and track in particular respond well to this process. It sets an intention for achievement, removes doubt and worry, and sets the energy for success.

You, too, can use the Walk-Through intention in many aspects of your life and work.

● *Try this:*

1. Set up by doing the grounding visualization on page 25.

2. Visualize the exact location where the event (meeting, presentation, etc.) will occur. Use as much specific detail as possible. Make it a three-dimensional picture.

3. Walk through the entire event—moment by moment—from beginning to end. If any part of the event is optional, for instance, if input is required by another person or people, visualize the most optimum situation.

4. Draw a gold circle around the entire event including the location. Ground the circle and event to the center of the earth.

● ●

Energy Explanation for the Walk-Through Intention

Many intentions have unpredictable aspects or results. When your goal is something as personally well known as a session in court, a twenty-yard dash, or a piece you have practiced on the piano a hundred times, you have a much greater opportunity to visualize with great specificity. Creating a picture that is very "real" to the inventor is the most important aspect of setting an effective intention. When you have specific knowledge about every moment of the event, it is all the more tangible.

The walk-through provides a specific location and set of actions. All that remains to complete the successful result is to eliminate worry and ground the intention to the center of the earth.

The "I'm Ready" Intention

A former registered nurse started a business that provides CPR training and other health and safety-related services to Fortune 500 companies. Her business vision was to provide an effective service helpful to all employees in large organizations while creating financial abundance to feed her interest in travel and home ownership in the expensive San Francisco Bay Area. She had worked many long hours in her medical career, so she wanted to take a fair amount of personal time away from her business.

She created a way to maximize the effectiveness of her days in the office by bringing intense focus to her work. Two years after starting her business, Susan had created results so astounding that she was able to cut down her work schedule to just a few months of the year even though the business provided an essential service every business day.

Her intention-setting technique is simple and extremely powerful. She sits at her desk and says out loud, "I am ready for new clients today."

The executive assistant who works with this woman reports that the phone begins to ring almost instantly after Susan states this intention, and further, that it has worked successfully for more than a decade. It can work for you, too. Here's how.

● Try this:

1. Set up by doing the grounding visualization on page 25.
2. Decide what you want to accomplish and assign a time period (day, week, month, etc.).
3. Visualize the desired outcome and the time period in simple, positive language and pictures. Incorporate specific details like deadline date and time and the

essential elements of who is involved, what you want them to do or experience, and where and why you want the intention to happen.

4. Create a large trash bin in front of you. Begin to drain into the bin all of the negative thoughts that stand in the way of achieving your desired goal. This can include worries ("I really, really *want* this but I know that it cannot *possibly* be done."), other people's invalidation ("My best friend says that I do not have enough experience to make this happen."), or any other negative or distracting thinking such as "This will take too much time (or money, or the right connections) so I might just as well give up right now!"

   All of these and many more types of negative thoughts focus energy away from the intention and rob it of essential "juice" to make it manifest in the world. It can be distracting to list all of the negative thoughts, so you might wish to "see" them instead as a cluster of brown, black, or gray energy that flows into the trash bin and through it all the way to the center of the earth where it disintegrates. If the dumpster fills up, dissolve it and visualize another one to continue the process.

5. When the negative thoughts stop flowing, dissolve the trash bin.

6. Bring the intention into the space before you. Picture yourself attaining the goal or visualize the words describing your goal in front of you.

7. Intuit or ask if any changes can be made to the intention to strengthen it and improve the likelihood of success. Make any necessary changes.

8. Bring the intention to a bright gold color. Create grounding for your intention—see it as a line of energy that is a strong connection from the bottom of the intention to the center of the earth. Complete the process by drawing a protective gold bubble around the intention and its grounding.

9. Move your intention to a comfortable place within your conceptual universe. Be inspired by it, "keep it in mind" to help you focus your creative energy until the intention happens.

• •

Energy Explanation for the "I'm Ready" Intention

Why does the "I'm Ready" intention work? Because the intender really *is* ready at the precise moment that the statement "I'm ready for new clients today" is made. You have already done the most important part of the work—removed all roadblocks that could sabotage the intention.

It is easiest to do this if you are completely convinced that your product or service is good or even excellent, that it is sold at a fair price, and that both you and the client will benefit from the transaction. If you also truly believe that you and your business deserve success, so much the better. In other words, when you remove all negative thoughts about the goal, you create a distilled intention without distracting negativity. There are no "hooks" (not smart enough, not enough time, not enough money, etc.) on which your creative strength can get caught up. Therefore it is all focused on the goal, and the energy floodgates open to buoy your intention and ground it into manifestation in the physical world.

At the end of the process I recommend that you bring the picture to a shiny gold color. This is because gold has a high energetic frequency that automatically elevates visualizations and intentions to their highest integrity and effectiveness. Coloring your visualization gold and grounding it strongly into the earth are powerful activities that enable project success.

The "Bring It On" Intention

There are times when you do not know what you want to create and you have neither the time nor the desire to go through the internal brainstorming process to create a specifically stated intention. Yet you know you want to create. You are very clear on that point.

At these times you can pose the question or puzzle that you wish to solve and then open the process to your Smart Spot. A very creative friend uses this process frequently to create unusual and interesting results. A person who is often bored with "regular life," he enjoys the unpredictable quality of what he draws to himself with this process. He calls it "Bring it on!" and because of the unpredictability of the serendipitous results, I agree that the name fits.

● *Try this:*

1. Set up by doing the grounding visualization on page 25.
2. Pose the question or puzzle you wish to solve.
3. Affirm that you are completely committed to the most appropriate result.
4. Visualize a wave of your creative energy flowing over and consuming the words of the stated puzzle.
5. Ground the visualization.

◦ ◦ ◦ ◦ ◦ ◦ ◦ ◦ ◦ ◦ ◦ ◦ ◦ ◦ ◦ ◦ ◦ ◦

Energy Explanation for the "Bring It On" Intention

Commitment and enthusiasm automatically feed creative energy, focus, and grounding into any intention. As one VP said, "The second-best solution that has your full commitment is always better than a first choice without backing." In energy terms, passion creates an energy vortex that attracts inventive ideas and others' enthusiasm. Virtually any solution in this situation will become manifest in the world.

When you care about the result and are excited enough by it to feed it and ground it, you create a physical world "thoughtform"—a force in the physical world. Manifestation follows.

* * * * * * * * * * * * * * * * * * * *

Visualization 3

Set an Effective Intention

1. Get grounded using the grounding visualization on page 25 to prepare to access your intuition:

   - Get calm
   - Breathe
   - Enter the Smart Spot
   - Ground

2. Set an intention by using one of the techniques described in this chapter or one of your own invention. Ensure that the intention is:

   - Specific
   - Believable
   - Measurable
   - Exciting to you

3. Bring the intention into the space before you. Visualize it in as much detail as possible. See it, hear it, make it real. Make it as three-dimensional as you can. Picture

yourself attaining the goal or visualize the words describing your goal.

4. Intuit or ask if any changes can be made to the intention to strengthen it and improve the likelihood of success. Make any necessary changes.

5. Make the intention a bright gold color. Create grounding for your intention—see it as a line of energy that is a strong connection from the bottom of the intention to the center of the earth. Complete the process by drawing a gold bubble around the intention and its grounding.

6. Shrink the picture of your grounded, protected intention down to about six to twelve inches and keep it with you in a place just outside your colored energy bubble where you will be inspired by it all day.

A Simple Analogy

You have now created an effective intention-to-be.

Let's revisit the H₂O (water) example briefly mentioned in the introduction to sum up how this works.

Think of the prenatal intention—your original idea—as steam, the gaseous or etheric form of H_2O, water. As you increase the amount of energy you give the idea, the etheric form becomes denser—similar to the liquid version of H_2O. When you ground the still-forming "watery" idea, you create even more solidity because of its connection to the earth.

Earth is where the action is! Earth energy is the quintessential element of the physical world. Connecting to this manifestation of energy through the grounding mechanism transports your idea fully into the physical plane. At this point, the idea has been transformed into a full-fledged, grounded intention.

Virtually everything in our universe has the ability to change appearance and functionality. Our quantum world is one of possibility, where everything changes from moment to moment. As you have learned in this chapter, creating the change you want requires that you (1) know what you want, and (2) set an intention to create it.

Now learn how to flesh out your intention with detail and enthusiasm in Chapter 4, Access Your Creative Intuition.

● *Exercises*

1. The next time you want to accomplish something, go through the deliberate process of setting an effective intention. Notice if the outcome is different from how it has been in the past when you did not set an intention.

2. Try setting an intention before attending a collaborative meeting. Were you able to stay more focused on the goal? Did others notice your intention and work toward it? How else was the collaborative process affected?

Ideas Presented in This Chapter

- An intention is a deliberate decision to create something.
- The best way to direct the enormous power of your creative strength is by setting effective intentions.
- Intention setting requires that you know what you want and that you use a deliberate process to create it and ground it in the physical world.

- The vision statement is a business's most powerful intention. It sets the energy around everything that happens in your organization by providing direction for priorities and policies.
- How often have I intentionally set goals in the past?
- In what situations do I usually set intentions and in which am I less inclined to do so?
- When I feel that things have "happened" to me or my department, is it because someone else has set the intention?

My Intention for Setting an Effective Intention

Spend a few minutes thinking about how you would like to use the concept of effective intention setting to improve your life or your work. Write your intention below:

4

Step 3: Access Your Creative Intuition

Grounding and Setting an Effective Intention lead to the third step in the Smart Spot process—Access Your Creative Intuition.

When you are grounded and have developed an effective intention, it is possible to bring your idea to manifestation on the physical plane. What the natal intention requires is regular feedings, just like a human baby, to grow and get strong so that one day it can make it on its own in the world. The "food" the intention needs is creative energy.

What Is Creative Intuition?

Creative intuition is your innate ability to create everything in your life and in your work—ideas, activities, relationships, and projects. Intuition is also your inborn skill to perceive the world around you. Almost everyone perceives information in the form of sound, pictures, feelings, and "knowing." This is the language of intuition.

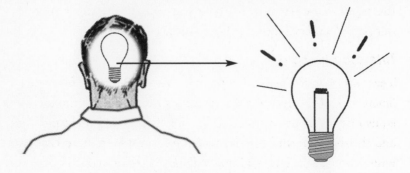

Infuse your intention with creative energy

Intuition—the Energy Explanation

We have said that energy is comprised of points of pulsating light that are constantly in a state of change. The organizing principles are the "language" of this energetic quantum state and are intellectually understandable to physicists and theoretical mathematicians. They can also be directly translated into musical notation and some other esoteric scientific "languages."

As great as it is that those who traffic in scientific theory have access to the information structure of the universe, it is most exciting to me that this "source" information is available to all of us through our creative intuition.

Each of us can direct and work with the source of these changes in creative energy through our intuition. Seeing the physically unseen, hearing the physically unheard, feeling, and "knowing" permits communication with the building blocks of the energy that creates the world anew moment by moment.

Intuition is the body's translation of the ultimate "source code"! When you learn to develop and trust your creative intuition, you open yourself to the possibilities of not just being able to *receive* information, but to have *input* to the energy source as well. It is this input that enables us to create our experience, our lives, and our projects every moment of every day.

Intention Is Input

The most powerful method of input is to set an intention from your Smart Spot. This method is effective because intention is the energy equivalent of a goal distilled to its most basic and potent picture and clearly states the objective with a measurable result. It is not a wish, a hope, or a dream, although it may be accompanied by these human emotions.

Intention setting can be done without great intuitive awareness. You are already setting intentions that work today. When you access your creative intuition by way of your Smart Spot, however, you can create even bigger and more complex projects, goals, and manifestations. Your idea might even change the way in which people experience life.

Creative intuition is the language or conduit for stating questions that need to be answered for your intention to be a success and for access to never-before-seen methods, processes, and inventions. Your creations are more intentional when you invent in the context of this information, which is not available through analytical methods.

Although analysis is appropriate for many mundane decisions we make each day, research and analysis alone cannot create a visionary result or innovative answer to the really big questions like "Should the company merge with our biggest competitor?" With such questions we often feel that we are blindly stumbling down an unknown path toward a goal about which we are uncertain. This is because we have been taught to use mental analysis to provide every answer. But this method doesn't work very well when creating a project or plan the size of which may change the world. Creative intuition is the only path to effective decisions of this type. Tapping in to the huge storehouse of information available by using your intuition every day significantly eases the way in business and in life. It also makes day-to-day working and living much more interesting.

I often hear the belief that you either are or are not intuitive, that it is a birth trait that is the luck of the draw, like brown hair or green eyes. Like all beliefs, this is self-fulfilling, because you tell yourself "I was not born intuitive, so I must make up for it by making decisions and plans based on my intellect and deductive reasoning." The more you believe that, the more you build upon your analytical skills and in the process neglect developing your innate ability to creatively, intuitively sense and fashion your environment.

You Were Born Intuitive

It is common to think of intuition as a set of perception abilities. The idea is widespread that these abilities are available to a fortunate few who are clairvoyant or have some mysterious skill like ESP (extrasensory perception). This does describe one aspect of intuition, yet creative intuition as defined in this book is much more than that.

In truth, everyone is innately intuitive; however, most people have such fleeting experience with it that it is dismissed as coincidence.

If you have ever predicted that someone was going to contact you or known what song was going to be played next on the radio, you have experienced using your intuition. These examples are just the tip of your creative intuition. Insight can create empires (or destroy them), generate ideas that change the world, and make your product or service irresistible, among many other things.

We all have a natural ability to perceive, invent, and manifest what we want. It comes from our inborn ability to sense our environment in a profound way. Although some people know from an early age that they sense things other people do not, or can see light or images that appear to be out of the ordinary, most of us need to develop our intuition in order to believe we have it. We need (or believe we need) tangible proof—hearing, seeing, knowing—that the information has been received into our awareness.

All it requires is the ability to get to the Smart Spot and a willingness to use the mind in a new way. Let's take a closer look at what creative intuition is and how it is manifested.

A Closer Look at Creative Intuition

Intuition is a component of your natural human ability to sense your environment and extract useful information through that sensing. At its most developed it is more than a sensing process—it is a creative mechanism to generate solutions, plans, and revolutionary ideas.

Intuition is an important part of the range of information available to us. This range encompasses instinct on the low end and creative intuition at the upper extreme. Instinct and intuition are on opposite ends of the information/creation spectrum because they come from different parts of the brain, use a dissimilar process, and are manifested differently.

We can measure intuitive power on a continuum that looks like this:

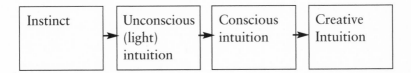

Each aspect of this system operates from a unique set of assumptions and skills different from reason, analysis, or mental thinking as shown in the following table.

Characteristics of Instinct vs. Intuition

Instinct	Creative Intuition
Response is automatic.	Response is germane, contextual, and often immediate.
Predictable response to stimulus.	Unique response appropriate to all aspects of a particular situation.
Repeatable exactly as done every other time.	Always available, always a unique solution.
Only one option.	Unlimited options.
Eliminates overwhelm by reducing choices.	Eliminates overwhelm (when grounded) by immediate synthesis of huge amount of data.
Effective if situation has exactly the same characteristics as previously encountered.	Effective in any situation or context.
"I've been here before and know exactly what to do—no questions asked."	"This situation is unique, and I will create a solution that takes all aspects into account."
Information amount and level is very low. There is a sense that just one smell, one look, one sound makes this situation exactly like any other that smells, looks, or sounds like it.	Information amount and level is very high—experienced through intuitive sight, hearing, knowing, or sensing.
Problem: No two situations are exactly alike and instinctive response may be inappropriate or even dangerous.	Challenge: It takes time to reach this level of skill. Once there, this process works well in any situation.

Human intuition is a range of awareness extending from the "natural instincts" of people and animals through several developmental stages until we attain the power to know and create in a constant energetic flow.

The thing that sets this continuum apart from other information gathering and creative activity is that *it is not analytical.*

Instinct: The "Smart Animal" Response

We say that an animal "knows" to blink or close its eyes when a bright light is shined on its face. This reaction protects the capability for light-sensitivity of delicate ocular tissue and prolongs the life of the species by protecting vision because most wild animals' sight is crucial to survival.

Instinct is the inborn tendency to behave in a way characteristic of a species. It is a natural, unlearned, predictable response to stimuli. So although there is no analytical thinking involved in instinctive reactions, there is also no creativity involved. It is similar to water running down a hill in a deep trench or gully that was cut into the hillside from such flows in the past. Even after a drought lasting many months or years, the next time water runs down the hill it is attracted uncontrollably into that same deep schism in the earth.

Instinct is an automatic, predictable reaction to stimuli. In this way, it can be argued that instinctive behavior is an inhibitor to creativity because the brain's neurological pathways have been so entrenched with a familiar reaction that a new, inventive response is impossible or nearly so.

Intuition: The Creative Evolutionary Process

Intuition, on the other hand, is very creative and falls on the other end of the information (reaction/creation) spectrum. Like instinct, human intuition also does not involve conscious thinking. Intuition goes many steps further than instinctive reaction in that it can be accessed *immediately but not automatically.*

The intuitive person instantly receives information that is comprehensive and contextual—it is not simply one predictable reaction to a stimulus, rather it is a fully formed thought or solution based upon all of the requirements and subtleties of the situation.

It is as if you had a staff of ten hardworking geniuses whose only job was to research the situation for as long as it took to understand the needs of everyone involved and all of the options for a solution—both obvious and hidden. Their job is to give you a comprehensive report that states everything they have learned and a brief summary that distills everything down to an elegant solution. If this staff of ten did all of that and instantaneously provided the perfect answer, that would approximate creative intuition.

Intuition is a manifestly creative process. On input, intuition can provide uncannily accurate and useful information. On output, it can create wildly creative solutions and plans. Several extremely intuitive people may get a similar "hit" when sensing information about a situation. This is the "input" (perception) side of intuition.

On the "output" (creation) side, those same creative people will probably come up with many different appropriate solutions, even though their perception of the situation is similar.

When you are using your own intuition or working with intuitive people, you know you are working with accurate information, but you never know which fabulous result will present itself. What could be more exciting?

Eureka! Inventing Your Idea

The most insignificant events can stimulate an intuitive solution. How many times have you heard about someone (or experienced for yourself) getting an "aha!" while eating dinner or taking a bath? Perhaps the most famous situation of this type occurred around 250 B.C. The mathematician Archimedes entered his bathtub one day while preoccupied with finding a way to determine the proportion of real gold to ordinary metal in King Hiero's crown. The task was to discover whether the crown was made of pure gold or some cheap imitation. At the time, the weight of gold per unit volume was well known, but given the intricate nature of the crown's design, it was impossible to measure its true gold content.

Archimedes noticed that the lower he sank into the tub, the higher the water rose, until it overflowed, and he experienced a revelation. He suddenly realized he could measure the volume of gold in the crown by simply dunking it in a tub filled to the brim, then measuring the water that overflowed.

He leaped from his tub and ran naked into the street hollering "Eureka!" Archimedes had discovered the law of specific gravity and the general science of hydrostatics.

The Greek expression "Eureka!" means, "I have found it!" and has come to epitomize the moment of inspiration, the instant in which something new is born.

A modern-day inventor whom you will meet below uses a similar approach. He familiarizes himself with all aspects of a technical problem he wants to solve and then "just goes about normal life"—reading email messages, noticing the new display in the flower shop window on his way home, or making himself aware of a friend's thinking process over lunch. He has done this for many decades, and he knows that eventually one of those mundane situations will yield a link, a connection, to a great idea that could solve the technical problem working in the back of his mind.

In this same way, you can posit your question, "I need a new sales manager for my department," or even, "I am ready for a new job," and then let the events of your regular life come into your awareness—connecting and interconnecting with situations in the context of creative energy.

An Inventor's Creative Intuition Process

The way each of us uses his or her intuition is as unique as the creator. An inventor describes his creative intuition process below.

Clarkston Douglas is an inventor, engineer, and Ph.D. in process management. He is also the founder and owner of a company that has evolved over twenty-five years from hardware inventions to patent writing and continuation engineering. He started out thirty years ago on project teams that developed office equipment at Xerox Corporation. He uses his intuition to fix problems with existing products and create new inventions.

Clarkston Douglas talks about his intuitive process:

I invent from necessity. When a vendor's equipment does not work properly, I get a clear idea of what is not working. I spend as much time as needed to analyze it because a clear statement of the requirements is critical.

Then I just go about my days, which usually consist of working on other projects already in motion, reading email and other information from the Web, and talking with customers and suppliers. I notice things going on around me. Sometimes something comes into my awareness that was always there, but for some reason didn't catch my attention in that particular way until just then.

The solution often comes from this objective observation of the world around me. Sometimes I analyze the things that are wrong with the present design and incorporate the ideas that caught my attention that day.

The most interesting way to solve it is with a premonition! The premonition comes out of nowhere—out of left field. It is an idea that includes all details of the design from concept all the way down to the best choice for materials. I like premonitions because they are interesting and so complete in detail.

If you have been around someone who operates from this creatively intuitive place—his or her Smart Spot—you know that they think and decide differently from most of us and are usually enthusiastic about their ideas. Many intuitive people also implement their ideas with ease (although this is a distinctly separate step in the intuitive process and requires its own set of skills).

A good, working definition of *creative intuition* is "the natural aptitude to directly know or learn of something and to create without the conscious use of reasoning."

Intuition provides immediate understanding through the apprehension of huge amounts of information and the ability to instantly synthesize it into actionable form.

Practicing Creative Intuition

You can learn how to access your creative strength by developing intuitive awareness. Creative intuition is an expansion upon the simple visualization method you used in Chapters 2 and 3. When you focus your attention on your subtle energy body's perceptions, you operate from insight and creativity.

Intuitive Perception Modes

What is the "right" way to receive information about your intention? That depends on the way your body naturally collects data. Note that whichever mode comes naturally to you is already at play. All you need to do is access the information encoded in it by operating from your Smart Spot. Let's look at the different ways the senses perceive intuited results.

Visual

Many people are visual. They may doodle on a notepad while they are on the phone. They may even be artists who paint or draw or throw pots in their leisure time or as a vocation.

In meetings and in everyday life these folks pull out a pad and pen when they explain something. They draw diagrams, create charts, and sketch arrows in every conceivable direction on the paper, flipchart, or whiteboard as they speak. If you have been on the receiving end of a conversation like this, you probably know that the drawing is not being done for you. In the end, the speaker might even throw the picture away. The drawing is often not understandable, but because the visual person "thinks" in images, he or she communicates best when pictures are at hand.

Visual people often talk in a language full of imagery. They may enjoy colors and shapes and ask you to retrieve the "blue binder with the yellow inserts from the messy bookcase," ask if you "see" what they mean, invite you to "look at it this way," or state the ultimate truth as "seeing is believing."

I know an IEEE engineer who is extremely intuitive. He sees problems and questions schematically as flowcharts, and the answer often appears to him like the blueprint of an electrical system. This is another type of visual orientation.

A commercial artist I know has many unique ways of viewing intuitive information. Nearly every time she explains an intuitive event, the pictures are completely different from the time before. The images can be computer icons, 3-D graphics, or even a group of pictures that tell a story like the frames of a newspaper cartoon.

A consultant attends many conferences and gives lots of speeches. He shares his great experience and insight about the industry through PowerPoint presentations that he creates on his computer. Not a power typist, this man distills his thinking through the process of seeing key words arrayed on the page, creating a structure or outline for his thoughts, and inserting pictures and graphs to illustrate ideas.

If you are visually oriented your intuitive information will prob-ably be received as pictures or drawings, short movies, computer-ized images, or holographs.

Auditory

Some people are auditory. They may be very sensitive to sounds and will pick up on background music or noise that the visually oriented or others may not have heard at all.

Auditory people speak a language full of sounds. They may be poets who enjoy the "mouth feel" of words. They may get pure pleasure from the way words sound. Auditory people often love to tell stories and listen to music and may be singers, musicians, or musically inclined.

They say things like "hear me out!" or "it sounds to me like you are saying . . . ," or "I hear ya!" They are the ones most likely to encapsulate an entire meeting by quoting a key statement. They may remember entire conversations word-for-word and (sometimes annoyingly) can repeat back exactly what you said on a specific occasion.

A popular recording artist, singer, and songwriter receives intu-itive information in a powerful and unique way. She hears music—popular songs, symphonic or opera—in answer to her questions. She finds that particular pieces of music provide a vast amount of nonverbal information, although the results can be literal. She offered to help a friend decide which of the three cities his com-pany was considering relocating him to would be best for both his career and his personal life. She clearly heard Tony Bennett singing "I left my heart in San Francisco." The client had visited and loved the city years ago and had always wanted to live there.

Based upon her intuited "hit," he moved to the Bay Area and in the process of creating a life he loved changed careers and found a new community, charitable work, and a partner. The historic accuracy of his intuitive friend's perception helped him to accept the information with comfort and certainty. His commitment to making a life work in San Francisco greatly facilitated success.

There is evidence that sound delivers powerful messages. You may have heard of the Mozart Effect®. Don Campbell developed the concept and has written nine books that reveal how music is an essential tool for health, intelligence, and well-being. He has lectured and taught all over the world to introduce his theory that music and the arts improve memory and awareness and activate creativity.

There are many other people and groups who use and explore the power of sound as an information source and a creative modality.

If auditory, you may receive intuitive information in the form of popular songs, symphonic or opera music, spoken words, tones, or sound effects. Once you get used to it, sound prints can provide a rich understanding.

Insight

You may know someone who operates from the intuitive state of insight. These people often produce the right answer on the spot, not knowing where it comes from and not seeing the need to defend it.

The engineering vice president for a Fortune 100 manufacturing company is known to sit quietly in new product launch meetings. No matter how volatile the discussion becomes, he observes everything from his inconspicuous location in the room. After everyone else has weighed in on the topic he offers an opinion. It is nearly always a "big picture" comment that overrides and yet considers the minutiae. Because the earlier part of the meeting was spent with others wrangling over details, the quiet calm with which he delivers the result is like stepping into a refreshing pool on a steamy day.

He is known to have "the cool voice of reason" in these meetings. Nearly always it is his opinion that becomes the decision of choice. His perception and ability to synthesize comprehensive and creative solutions make him a valuable member of the team. Yet he has a great sense of perspective about his ability. He trusts his skill (as do others), yet he knows that it is most available to him when he opens his awareness and is objective and emotionally impartial about the outcome. As a result, he is one of the best-liked people in the company.

People who "just know" the right thing to do or who "understand" without analysis the deep implications of complex issues may receive intuitive information through insight. It is often accompanied by a calm demeanor and a grounded orientation.

Insight is "knowing" in a high state of understanding and usefulness. It provides answers that often have the appearance of words of wisdom. A client once told me he had received the same answer each time he accessed his intuition and he wanted to know how to get a better reply. I asked what the answer was. He said he had been told that "there is not one right answer. Choose any one. Put your heart and energy into it. It will succeed."

We worked together to align him in a calm, intuitive decision-making space. He clearly sensed the correctness of each option and, knowing that he could not choose badly, was able to select one and commit the necessary enthusiasm and resources. Because he dropped all other selections and gave full support to his choice, I was not surprised to learn that the project was a success.

If your intuition provides insight, you may receive wise, "big-picture" answers that display great depth and a broad understanding.

Feeling

We all know people who operate on feelings. They may stride from meetings in high emotion or get passionately behind a point of view or plan of action. Sometimes we say these people are sensitive because they may have strong reactions to individuals or situations that are benign to everyone else.

Feeling language is filled with descriptions of emotion and sensation. These people "feel" that the new plan can be more successful than it appears, they may experience the new VP as a "pain in the neck" (or other body part), or their hearts may race at unexpected news. These are the people most likely to literally "feel your pain."

Feeling people may sense the intuitive hunch as a "gut reaction." This is a churning, punch, or otherwise unambiguous reaction in the lower abdomen. Some people feel harmed by it (they usually perceive the "gut reaction" as negative), and others look forward to it because it confirms decisions made with analytical thought.

An advertising executive called for a presentation to decide among five final designs for the new campaign for their biggest client. The first three designs were interesting and attractive. One was even amusing. The moment the storyboard was unveiled on the fourth choice she got a very strong physical reaction: "I had a great sense of euphoria as the curtain went up on number four. Even before hearing the dialogue, it certainly appeared to be the most promising. I did listen to the entire presentation but I wasn't surprised that in the end the fourth was the clear winner."

If your intuition is felt through emotion or other physical body response, your mode is feeling.

Caution: Feeling is the murkiest form of accessing intuition because it is most easily clouded by your own emotion, others' feelings, or distractions. This is because it is sensed lower in the body where our intuition can be less reliable. If possible, try to get a second opinion for feeling-based intuition. This confirmation may come through visual or auditory intuition or through insight.

Intuition Visualization Table of Results

Mode	Intuitive Method
Visual	Pictures, drawings, movies, computerized images, holographs, schematics.
Auditory	Music (popular songs or symphonies, concertos, opera, etc.). Spoken stories, tones, printed words, sound effects.
Insight	"Knowing." Big-picture answers that may appear as words of wisdom.
Feeling	"Gut reaction," discomfort, euphoria, excitement, other emotion, or other physical body response.

Do you get the impression that any way that you receive information is OK? Great! You have the right idea.

The following visualization will help you to access your creative intuition.

• • • • • • • • • • • • • • • • • • •

Visualization 4

Access Your Creative Intuition

1. Get grounded. Use the grounding visualization on page 25 to prepare to access your intuition:

   - Get calm
   - Breathe
   - Enter the Smart Spot
   - Ground

2. Set an intention that is:

- Specific
- Believable
- Measurable

3. Open yourself to freedom. Feel the enormous expanse of calmness in the Smart Spot. Gently move obstructions away to give you a full 360-degree view. The vista is similar to that from the top of a lighthouse, the bridge of the Starship *Enterprise,* or the top of Mount Everest. This is a place without boundaries, without rules, without restriction. This is a place of supreme freedom.

4. Enter objectivity. Bring to your mind's eye the color of a beautiful white pearl. Notice the gleam of its creamy luster. Add a bright, shiny gold like that found in jewelry. Know that this pearl white with gold color is the energy setting for objectivity. You can also access objectivity by setting an intention to be in this neutral space. Allow your emotions, beliefs, and those of others involved in the project to dissolve and travel out of your energy space through your grounding. As you set these and other body feelings aside, let your mind soar. Explore options never before seen. Expand into the freedom around you.

5. Pose the question. When you feel ready, imagine your intention in the space before you. Let the question sit there without judgment or opinion. See it as if from a mountaintop—a faraway presence that is mildly interesting and does not require any emotion or reaction.

6. Wait. Allow the intention's energy to incubate in the quiet space you have created. You may sense an answer right away. Sometimes you will need to wait a bit while the question aligns with the opening for the answer to slip through to you. Try not to fill the wait by conjuring an answer or setting an expectation that it will come out in any particular way.

7. Sense the answer. The answer may come in visual form like a short movie, a photograph, or computerized image. You might hear a song or someone explaining the answer. The response often comes as "knowing" the best option. Trust the way you receive the response. Intuition is as unique as your fingerprint or voiceprint, and operates best when you trust the way you receive information.

8. Get clarification. If the answer is unclear, reaffirm your grounding, reposition your awareness in the Smart Spot, and restate the pearl white with gold color. Ask again. Wait. Receive the answer. If you want additional detail, pose a follow-up question.

9. Come back into the room. When you feel that the process is complete, slowly open your eyes and become aware of your surroundings.

Note: With practice you will be able to access your intuition while you are on the phone, in a meeting, or other places outside your protected, quiet space.

Ground Your Creative Intuition

By now you have experienced how important it is to create and maintain your own personal grounding. You have also grounded your ideas and intentions to keep them from being invalidated by others or buffeted by changeable situations.

It is just as important to ground your creative intuition ability and it is important for precisely the same reasons. When a person, object, idea, or situation is grounded, it is shielded from the whims and emotion of others and remains strongly focused on its intention.

One way to know if your intuition is not grounded is that your perception and creation abilities lose focus and become diffuse or you feel physical discomfort while attempting to access your intuitive ability.

Grounding your intuition is simple. Imagine a grounding cord beginning at your Smart Spot and traveling through your physical body down to the center of the earth. You experience your intuition from this spacious place of awareness, and when it is grounded, your perception increases and your creativity is energized.

In the intentional intuition model so far, you have grounded yourself, selected the most appropriate idea or goal, and visualized it in detail. Continue to create ever more well-defined and sharper details and to make three-dimensional every aspect of the intention-to-be.

Feed the concept with your creative energy to give it its own generation engine, and as it gets stronger and sharper, start to move it outside of your head and into your aura. Your aura defines your energy arena. It is a bubble that extends about two to three feet all around you, containing both your energy body and your physical body.

The stronger the intention-to-be becomes, the clearer the visualization, and the farther it moves from the intuitive center of your head, your Smart Spot. When it reaches the outermost edge of your aura and moves outside of your energy field, it begins to take on a life of its own.

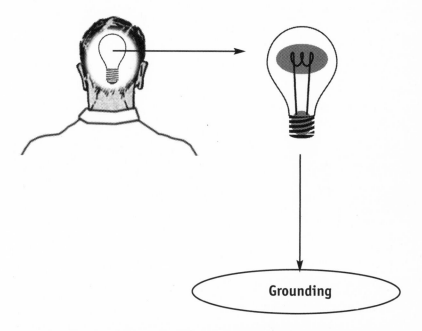

Move the intention outside your aura

At this point the intention requires its own grounding because it is no longer part of your physical body's Earth connection. Grounding the intention is as simple as visualizing an energy structure—a cord—that begins at the bottom of your intended picture or movie and connects sturdily into the center of the earth.

The intention is already beginning to assume an earth presence because of its grounding, but it is important to continue to feed it with your creative energy and imagination. This means that it still resides within your *conceptual universe.*

Your conceptual universe encompasses everything that you can specifically visualize or otherwise imagine. It is easy to "see" with your physical eyes a flower sitting on a table in front of you. It is also easy to see it on a table across the room if you have direct line of sight.

It requires visualization to imagine it on a table in the next room or in the building across the street, yet it takes no more imagination—just a slightly different visualization—to think of it sitting on a table in Tokyo or London.

As long as you have a clear picture or sense of the intention, it does not matter how far away it is from your physical body. It is still within your conceptual universe—that area in which you conceptualize or visualize the picture.

At this stage your idea becomes a full-fledged intention. Continue to give your new intention energy. Watch the picture come into extremely sharp focus. If it is not already three-dimensional,

You have created an effective intention

visualize it with a front, back, sides, top, and bottom. Give it weight and texture and substance. Involve as many senses as you can to make the natal intention "real" to you.

Your intention is now a holograph—a three-dimensional energetic picture of the future.

Still feeding creative energy to your intention, project slightly into the future and notice how the manifested goal is received in the physical world. How do people react to your creation? What happens after it is manifested? Is that what you wanted to happen or would you like to modify your intention to encompass a more-refined goal?

Consider all aspects of an important intention—before, during, and after—in as much detail as possible. In this way, you will create what you really want.

● *Exercises*

1. The next time you set an agenda for a meeting, create or update a project plan, or prepare a presentation, try using your creative intuition as the driving force. Take a moment to ground and access your Smart Spot. Set an intention to solve the issue or invent something new by using your creative intuition. Notice if the project or solution is more appropriate to the need. Was the solution more or less obvious?

2. Notice how you felt about the solution or project mentioned above. Was it more "creative"? How did it feel to work this way? Did time pass more quickly? Was the process more enjoyable than usual?

Ideas Presented in This Chapter

- Creative intuition is your innate ability to perceive subtle information and to create whatever you want.
- Instinct is a predictable response to stimulus and in this sense is automatic. Intuition is the ability to synthesize comprehensive, appropriate results from a huge amount of perceived data.
- Intuition can be an immediate but not an automatic process.
- There are many valid ways to perceive intuitively. They are: visual, auditory, feeling, and "knowing."

Questions to Ask Yourself

- How comfortable am I with the idea that I am intuitive?
- In what situations have I used my creative intuition with intention?
- When have I collaborated creatively with others?

My Intention for Accessing My Creative Intuition

Spend a few minutes thinking about how you would like to use the concept of creative intuition in your life or work. Use the space below to write your intention.

5

. . . . *S*tep Four:
Act with
Intention

Grounding, intention, and creative intuition all lead to the culmination step in the Smart Spot process—Act with Intention.

What Is Intentional Action?

Intentional action happens when you feel confident with the results of the previous three steps in the process and proactively implement the solution. It is the step in which you act on these words, "We know the solution. Let's do it!"

Action is the implementation of an idea, plan, or solution. Effective action is realization. It is often the most exhilarating step in the Smart Spot process because everyone involved gets to see results take shape in the physical world.

Some examples of effective action with intention include:

- Implement a marketing plan.
- Launch a new product.
- Start an organization from scratch.

Act with Intention—an Energy Explanation

When you ground yourself and your intention and feed it with your creative energy you have made a very big statement in the subtle energy world. Your idea has developed to the hologram stage— that three-dimensional, imaginative structure that is the precursor to manifestation in the physical world. A viable hologram is the step just before action—when you send the manuscript to the publisher, step onto the playing field, or introduce your idea in the meeting.

It is critically important to do whatever action is necessary to implement that hologram. Why? If it does not continue to receive your commitment and creative energy, the hologram that you worked so hard to invent and achieve will disappear. Very quickly the creative points of light coalesced into the energetic form of your intention will scatter and dissipate. These universally available pulsating light beams are then unavailable to you in the original intention format. Eventually they will be reconstituted in a new form according to the architectural plan of another effective intention, which could be just fine, but an intention not acted upon is lost in that specific form forever.

Not acting with intention is one of the biggest stumbling blocks in the creative process. Fear of failure or of being overwhelmed by the personal responsibility required to achieve the goal are often cited as reasons a promising project was dropped just before it would have been manifested. What an enormous waste of creative effort! Every other step in the process has already been completed; all that is required is the physical step to get to the gym, pick up the phone, write the first sentence, or get on the plane.

When you act to deliberately implement your intention, you show the ultimate commitment. Momentum and follow-through are all-important in our changeable quantum world.

Act on your intention

Benefits of Acting with Intention

Action Grounds the Creative Process

It is important to ground your intention in order to give it weight—to take it from etheric, cloudlike dream form to a solid, stable Earth presence.

Earth is where the action is, and as we have learned, grounding engages the earth aspect—the physical component of manifestation. It is the catalyst that "matches" Earth energy to your intention visualization. In a truly amazing transformative process, the idea moves from intention to reality as you or the people in your organization take action on it.

Action Ensures Manifestation

Acting with intention amplifies the amount of universal creative energy available for manifestation. This happens because action creates momentum and energetic points of light are attracted to the excited state of energy molecules as they coalesce into a new product or a closed deal. The vortex formed by this uniting of energy is amplified as more and more points of light join the model. The form itself becomes increasingly dense until it is a physical product you can hold in your hand or deposit in your bank account.

Action Brings Your Intention into the Present Moment

A lot of the Smart Spot process is the creation of a future event or product. It is important to imagine how things might be different or what the eventual physical form of your invention will be in order to make it happen. We have seen that visualizing creates a thoughtform that, if fed with creative energy, will soon be able to be seen on Earth.

Even though projecting into the future is an important part of the process, it is critical that the energy form of the intention be set at the "right" place on the timeline for it to be manifested. The physical world is about *now*—it is what you see in front of you, hold in your hand, or ride to your destination. It is what we call reality.

An intention is a powerful energetic presence when it is well visualized and grounded, yet it is still a part of the subtle energy world until it appears on your doorstep, now, in the present moment.

Three Types of Intentional Action

There are three types of intentional action:

1. Act Immediately.
2. Research and analyze intuited solution to refine or justify action.
3. Engage in ongoing intuitive decision-making during the implementation process.

Let's examine each of these.

Act Immediately

The most straightforward way to use intentional action is to follow the basic Smart Spot plan. The Act-Immediately model looks like this:

1. Ground
2. Intend
3. Intuit
4. Act

Robin Toft, CEO, Roy Toft Photography, says it best: "In the corporate world the step after the intuited hit, the *feeling*, was to go back and create a plan with all of the numbers so that everyone could see that it was a good idea. Now that I am CEO of my own business I just say, 'I want to do this,' and get right to work."

Or as the Nike advertisements encourage: "Just do it!"

As we discussed earlier, a business vision statement is a very clear intention. In Critical Issue "Building a Collective Vision" (NCREL, 1995), author Kent Peterson (University of Wisconsin, Madison) references W. G. Bennis and B. Nanus (Leaders: The Strategies for Taking Charge, 1985) and observes that acting with intention is not a single-task practice:

> A . . . vision can easily stagnate. Therefore, it must be regularly expressed, proclaimed in word and deed, and communicated through mission statements, mottos, logos, and the behavior of formal and informal leaders. The mission should be reconsidered on a regular basis, incorporating changes and additions to reflect new circumstances, new opportunities, or new goals. . . . Both formal and informal leaders communicate their vision by how they spend their time, what they talk about, what problems they solve first, and what they get excited about. In every act, leaders reinforce the values they hold and the vision they hope to achieve.

The process of brainstorming and writing down the mission statement is one example of creative action. Posting it on a company bulletin board or website expands that action and puts even more energetic power behind the intention. In other words, more molecules of energy are activated in the vicinity of the mission statement when it is focused upon, reproduced, and disseminated. The increased energy surrounding the intention then attracts even more creative action. When a project starts out with enough intention and action, it practically becomes self-generating and self-fulfilling.

There are many ways to augment a mission statement's influence. One way is to consistently dedicate a portion of company meetings to discussing the mission statement's meaning and implementation. You might also wish to reproduce it in newsletters and catalogs, include it in whole or in part in customer correspondence, or print it on cards that accompany product shipments.

All of these actions and many others create interest in the intention expressed in the mission statement. Each of these activities elevates the energetic "oomph" surrounding your company's idea, mission, and products. Action elevates energetic impact. If your intention is to create interest in your product or service, act to make the intention known. Nothing is more effective.

Research and Implement

A second type of intentional action is to confirm and expand upon the "big-picture" solution with analytical research and development. The Research-and-Implement model looks like this:

1. Ground
2. Intend
3. Intuit the "big picture" solution
4. Research and analyze to support big picture
5. Visualize details
6. Creatively collaborate

7. Distribute group action items
8. Act on solution

Clarkston Douglas, the inventor whom we met in the previous chapter, uses a special way to test his intuition by following up on those inventions that appear as fully formed solutions he calls "premonitions." He says that these solutions "come out of nowhere and include the design all the way down to the best choice for materials."

The types of inventions that Douglas creates can be very expensive to implement in terms of design, testing time, and materials in manufacturing. In order to maintain his credibility and contracts with established companies, it is important that everything go like clockwork.

The stakes are high, so he uses an analytical backup-and-testing process to ensure that his intuited solution really is appropriately suited to the situation. He gets the intuited hit down on paper by writing down every step in the process including materials to be used, manufacturing required, and the operation of each part of the invention.

As he writes, he tests each aspect in his mind; then he tests statistically and, if necessary, tests in the laboratory. In other words, he analyzes and sends the intuited intention through the filters of his training and experience to test feasibility. He may already know from his intuition that the answer will work, but at what cost in implementation time, materials, and manufacturing process? An answer that is perfect operationally or solves the question elegantly but costs too much to implement is, in truth, not the perfect answer.

When a step or aspect of the intuited answer is outside of his experience, he conducts research into the material's tensile strength, heat resistance, longevity, or other attribute in books or on the Web. When necessary, he also does physical testing in the lab.

In this way he "reverse engineers" his intuited answer. He begins with a complete, fully functional solution and seeks to prove its manufacturability and effectiveness. As Douglas says, "As I write down each step, I research and test every material and task. Experience is a great help in determining the feasibility of the project."

As Andrew Krcik, Vice President, Marketing, PGP Corporation, explains, intuition can also be "reverse engineered" in other departments and divisions in organizations:

> Intuition gets you the most workable and often most creative answer. Analyzing massive amounts of data cannot in itself provide answers and often leads to the dread 'analysis paralysis.' The best answers come from the combination of experience and intuition.
>
> Once I know the answer, I use staff-work to support and explain my decision or recommendation. This is usually required as part of formal business planning processes and to satisfy the intellectual and analytical requirements of others. Most people think I get the answer from the research. In fact, I take a quick review of the materials, intuitively weigh the issue, and form a decision. Then I mine the available documents for materials that illuminate this decision.

This is a second way in which the Smart Spot process can be effective. We see it in engineering, manufacturing, and also in finance, marketing, and sales. The data and analysis portion of the creative act can follow and support the intuited "big picture" solution.

If we were to look at the Research-and-Implement method in light of the creator's personality or emotional experience during the process, we would see that imaginative ideas are visualized in the exhilaration of creative intuition, fleshed out with detail in a state of calm analysis, and implemented with enthusiastic action.

Intuit As You Go

Another way to create is to intentionally check in with your intuition at every step in the process. The Intuit-As-You-Go model looks like this:

1. Ground
2. Intend
3. Intuit
4. Test
5. Intuit
6. Develop
7. Intuit
8. Final Test
9. Decision
10. Act

Many people who value their intuition use it as an integral skill—part of the panoply of talents—to continuously test each step in the creative process. Trial lawyers are often extremely intuitive and use this integrated process of intuiting, testing, researching, testing, and intuiting again before getting to action.

If you have ever been a juror you may have seen the litigating attorneys' creative process. Each side makes opening remarks in which they interpret the legal question to their advantage—either pro or con. Balance is upset when opposing counsel refutes a key point. This imbalance can be almost palpable in the courtroom. A "continuance" to the next day is often requested when the blow has been particularly well targeted.

The next day the side that appeared as underdog in the previous court session may come in with a new idea and the evidence to support it. In some trials, particularly if they are high profile, this jockeying goes on day after day as each new, creative idea or spin on the topic is introduced and "evidence" is convincingly offered to support the concept and yield a jury decision in favor of their client. At every step there is need for revision or realignment of the goal so that the attorney is constantly acting on new, creative solutions in the trial litigation process.

The Intuit-As-You-Go model is especially visible in a dynamic selling situation. Spectacularly effective sales people have honed their innate intuition to a refined focus and insight. They are good listeners who are great at perceiving both verbalized and unstated needs. They sense the prospective client's requirements and are instantaneously able to synthesize a complete picture of the benefits of their product or service that exactly fits those requirements.

Most effective sales people are very good communicators, and if they are especially so, they generally also show this image to the prospect in a subtle "energy picture." In other words, they open up their own visualization to the prospective client. This picture might be a three-dimensional representation of the prospect enjoying the use of the product or service and either becoming a hero in the process or having so effective a result that they are freed up to do more important or more creative work.

Showing energy pictures or visualizations to others is a very powerful way to communicate. A picture really does say a thousand (or a million!) words. In the business world where we have boundaries about emotion and attempt to keep most conversations and negotiations in the realm of objective language and neutral feeling, visualizations can introduce the idea of enjoyment and satisfaction even as no one speaks those words.

Visualizing with insight and accuracy and showing those pictures to others with integrity are very creative acts. A well-timed and interesting persuasive conversation between an effective sales executive and a savvy client can sound a bit like the dialogue in a well-written play or movie. The following are examples of both traditional-selling and intuitive-selling dialogues.

Traditional Selling

Intuitive Selling

The effective sales person intuitively listens and senses the key aspects required for the selling process to continue. Then he or she creates a solution that answers the question or concern while it illuminates the product's benefits.

This means that sales people often spend much of their working day in full creative expression. Awareness and the creative ability to instantly synthesize workable solutions are important contributions to their success.

As you become skilled in accessing your intuition you may increasingly depend upon it to keep projects on track, clear your mind, and to create success.

How to Act with Intention

Use the following visualization to act upon your intention.

• • • • • • • • • • • • • • • • • • •

Visualization 5

Act with Intention

1. Get grounded. Use the grounding visualization on page 25 to prepare to access your intuition:

   - Get calm
   - Breathe
   - Enter the Smart Spot
   - Ground

2. Set an Intention that is:

   - Specific
   - Believable
   - Measurable
   - Exciting to you

3. Intuit the big-picture approach best suited to your
   intention:
   - Move to freedom and objectivity
   - Pose the question (intention)
   - Receive the answer

4. Act with intention:
   - Implement immediate action.
     or
   - Research and analyze to refine or justify action.
     or
   - Engage in ongoing intuitive decision making during
     the implementation process.

Act Now!

Whichever process you use, be aware that it is important to act on
your intuited creation. Why? Because energy follows thought, and
the more ideas you develop without implementing or otherwise dis-
mantling them, the more your energy is tied up in the creating state.
This means that there is less of your creative energy available to
design, develop, and implement new intentions.

The Role of Trust

There are many ways to use your intuition. Some of the executives
I know trust their ability to intuit the right advertising campaign
or to "know" the next strategic career move or to unerringly (or
practically so, in any case) "read" people.

Some CEOs say that they have such good reputations for being
right about their hunches that others in the organization have built
their careers and strategic plans around their ideas.

This type of validation builds trust in your own intuitive hits and
when you trust them and support them with right implementation
you achieve the trust of others in your organization. Right implementation includes really getting behind what you propose, and

learning to propose it to management and to your staff in a way that earns acceptance and enthusiastic action on the new idea.

The confidence that you and others place in you augments the trust you have in your intuition, and it becomes a success cycle—each part building on and playing off the other.

Trust and action work hand in hand and are integral aspects of the Smart Spot process.

● *Exercises*

1. The next time you want to accomplish something, act with intention. Notice if the outcome is different from what it has been in the past when you did not act with intention.
2. Can you identify your most favored type of intentional action? Do you prefer Act Immediately, Research and Implement, or Intuit As You Go?
3. In which situations do you prefer each of the three types of intentional action?

● ● ● ● ● ● ● ● ● ● ● ● ● ● ● ● ● ● ●

Ideas Presented in This Chapter

- Action is an essential part of the Smart Spot process because it is the time when the product, service, or idea is manifested.
- Action is reality in the present, now.
- Action brings the energetic thoughtform of your intention to its dense, physical form.

Questions to Ask Yourself

- How often have I acted with intention in the past?
- In what situations do I usually act and in which am I less inclined to do so?
- Am I reticent about taking action on my intentions? If so, why?

My Intention for Acting with Intention

Spend a few minutes thinking about how you would like to use the concept of acting with intention to improve your life or your work. Use the space below to write your intention.

6

The Next Step

If you have made it this far, you have covered a lot of ground. You have learned how to establish your grounding connection so that you can operate from your Smart Spot—the place of centered and calm wisdom. You learned to set an effective intention—the key to creating the energetic focus required to create what you really want. You explored both the perception and creative aspects of using your creative intuition. And you learned to act with intention to experience your manifestation in the real world.

The Smart Spot process is effective in a wide range of both business and personal situations. It is the deliberate act of deciding what you really want and being so committed to it that you are willing to create the energetic vortex necessary to bring your wildest imaginings to fruition.

If you will follow the ideas presented in this book, you will create intentionally.

Developing Consciousness

You have covered a lot of territory in a subject that may have been relatively (or even entirely) new to you when you first opened this book. These ideas and techniques portend a world of people, projects, and situations viewed through the enhanced awareness of your intuition.

To continue opening yourself to awareness, notice how people act and react to speech, activity, decisions, and one another. There is an energy component to everything that occurs. It is happening and will continue to happen whether you notice it or not, and with awareness you can tap in to the huge storehouse of information going on all around you. With time and practice you will learn to synthesize this data down to its most powerful essence and know it to be intuitive wisdom.

Perhaps you are looking for the next step in the process now that you know the basics to access your intuition. If so, there are many simple ways to extend your awareness and build trust and confidence in your intuited solutions.

Building Awareness

Energy information can be found in abundance all around you. To build your skill, consider beginning with awareness of your inter-personal communication. Watch what happens when you are in meetings or one-on-one conversations. How do people act? React? Can you get to an observer's stance to view the process? The more often you "tune in" to your awareness, the more cognizant you will become. You will start to notice ways in which you can modify your own communication and energy thought formation. Remember that energy follows thought, so if you set an intention to become more aware, you *will* be. The only follow-through required is to notice the world and the people around you.

Your Creative Intuition Is Always Available

The most important point in this book is that *you are intuitive* and have the great strength of your creative intuition available on-call at all times. Intuition visibly appears when it is recognized. All that is required is that to use your eyes, ears, feelings, and "knowing" to tune in to your environment and its subtle yet constant stream of information.

One of my clients manages several hundred employees in a technology company. She lives in Europe and has worked with me via phone, but learned to meditate on her own. When I called to ask if she would like to contribute a remark to this book she said,

> I don't meditate as much as I used to. In fact, I haven't sat and done it for several months. But I feel as if I am in an active intuitive state all of the time now. I get up in the morning and place myself in the Smart Spot and make sure I ground. I am aware of that and do it consciously, but then I don't actively set it up again during the day unless I encounter a difficult situation.
>
> If we start to have trouble communicating, I relax, breathe deeply, and try to get in touch with my connections. I make sure I am in my Smart Spot and try it that way. Sometimes I even close my eyes and get in touch with what I really know or feel about the situation. I do this when I want to be very accurate and not emotionally attached to what I'm talking about.
>
> The effect is that calm comes over both the conversation and the person I am talking with. A stronger connection happens in the communication. A better understanding.

You, too, can have a better understanding of the people and situations around you simply by establishing your grounding and operating with energetic personal responsibility.

There are times when all of us feel like we are "inside the problem" of financial stress, too many options, or not enough resources. These are very difficult times to make appropriate decisions. Instead of pushing through at a time like this, consider changing the situation by changing the energy. Ground yourself and set an intention for calm awareness. Perhaps you, too, will have the experience of feeling more like the cause of your actions instead of the effect.

Acting with Integrity

Awareness leads to personal responsibility. You wouldn't brush your teeth in the middle of a meeting or scream "You are a jerk!" in your manager's office (at least not under normal circumstances). Energy communication and energy management are just as important as learning to control emotion, language, and activity. It is just as essential to act in ways that are appropriate and effective in your world. People *do* sense and react to energy communication as much as or even more than they do words or body language. The workplace, like every part of life, has begun to notice these subtle levels and there is no turning back. Once you know that this occurs, your life is forever changed. Awareness creates accountability.

The Next Step

As powerful as the Smart Spot process is, it is just the beginning of the world of subtle energy knowledge. There are many people and organizations doing groundbreaking work on the topics of perception, creativity, and energy management.

I encourage you to follow your interest in these topics. Simply by virtue of your having acquired this book, you have established yourself as a member of the new creativity paradigm being created in the world today. This is not an organized movement in a normal sense. It is a loose collection of people interested in their own development and enlightenment and in that of all people and of Earth itself.

I welcome you and honor you as "one of us"—those who are willing to work for a better tomorrow.

If you feel very connected to the Smart Spot process described in this book, you may wish to consider seeking an intuitive consultation, attending a workshop, or finding further training to enhance your intuition. There are many good meditation teachers, practitioners, and schools across the country.

Consultations and workshops are listed on my website. I can also personally recommend the excellent technical approach and integrity of the teaching staff at the Academy of Intuitive Studies and Intuition Medicine® in Sausalito, California. Their fourteen-month Master of Intuition Medicine (MIM®) program includes hundreds of hours of supervised internship in addition to thought-provoking lectures, meditation practice, group and individual study, and work in learning labs. If you are unable to attend classes in Sausalito, you may also receive high-quality training through the AISIM® Distance Education Program or with Francesca McCartney's book and tape series, *Intuition Medicine, The Science of Energy.*

The Power of Your Intuition

I leave you with the words of my teacher. Michael McCartney lives in the real business world as an entrepreneur. He is also a visionary who never fails to inspire and explain the world in profound ways.

> My work is an action and an expression of my intuition. Every thought, concept, and visualization flows from my intuitive center. When I act without recognizing this information my actions and their results cannot be anticipated. Using my intuition keeps me in the moment and able to recognize my part of the problem from the whole. Using my intuition gives me the perspective to see the options in any situation and to be able to separate out the truth from the lie, the fictional and the emotional, the mental from the spiritual. Using my intuition I can see clearly my mistakes

and their root causes. By using my intuition I affirm my interconnectedness with humanity and all things.

This statement shows that it possible to pragmatically live in the world and to create and enjoy its abundance while operating with perspective and integrity. Perhaps we all know that ethical behavior in the physical world involves truth and good intention. Energetic integrity is just beginning to be explored. It is the root of ethical behavior and an expansion upon it.

Being grounded and containing your power within your own energy field is the ultimate integrity in the world of energy. It means that you are not imposing your will on another human being or on the planet.

Michael's statement shows that he uses his intuition for information, a sense of perspective, choosing appropriate options, and as a test for the skewing that emotion can cause in objective decision making. He assumes that his energy field is joined with that of all other people and as such is part of a great resource on the earth. As such, he understands his interconnectedness with people and all things.

This is a profound yet simple concept. We are responsible for what we create in the world and how we experience and manifest those creations.

You are the cause of your actions. What do *you* really want to create?

Glossary

Academy of Intuitive Studies and Intuition Medicine®—School founded by Francesca McCartney in Sausalito, California, to teach the concepts and techniques of Intuition Medicine®.

Act Immediately—Intentional action model in which the intuited solution is acted upon as soon as it is intuited.

action—Action is the fourth step in the Smart Spot process. It is the process by which the intuited or perceived intention is manifested on the physical plane.

auditory—Intuitive perception mode that focuses on the ability and propensity to "hear" with the physical ears or clairaudience (subtle energetic hearing) sounds, tones, and vibrations.

aura—The human energy field surrounding the physical body and the energy body. The aura appears as an egg-shaped bubble. Part of the body's energetic protection system.

awareness—The quality or state of being conscious, informed, or cognizant; the intention and ability to notice behavior and subtle energy feedback to expand perception.

big picture—Intuited solution that includes all details and processes of the intention.

"Bring It On" intention—Overview intention in which the question or puzzle is posed and the process opened up to one's creative subconscious. Sometimes creates unusual and unpredictable results.

colorize—The process of visualizing the filling of your personal energy field with a chosen color.

"Come into your body"—Expression that means aligning and moving your subtle energy body into your physical body and connecting the two aspects of yourself at the base of the spine. The physical body is the earthly "home" for your subtle energy body.

conceptual universe—The area in which you conceptualize or visualize an idea. As long as you have a clear picture or sense of the intention it does not matter how far away it is from your physical body. It is still within your conceptual universe.

consciousness—Awareness. Energetic or spiritual enlightenment.

creative intuition—Your innate ability to create everything in your life and work—ideas, activities, relationships, and projects. Intuition is also your inborn skill to perceive the world around you. Almost everyone perceives information in the form of sound, pictures, feelings, and "knowing." This is the language of intuition.

energetic integrity—This idea goes beyond the mental wish not to hurt someone or cause harm. It encompasses the concept of not interfering with others' free will—with their choice to operate as they wish in the world. Controlling others is not in energetic integrity.

energy—Catch-all phrase to connote the subtle universal concept that all things are composed of vibrating points of light that may be sensed by human perception and interpreted in a meaningful way.

energy body (also referred to as "your energy")—Your quintessential nature—your creative essence. Your energy body is the companion structure to every physical body born on Earth. In a very real sense, it is your life.

"Energy follows thought"—The idea that at a subatomic level every person, every thought, every sound, every thing is comprised of pulsating light that is in a constant state of change. Directing that change—creating a path for it to follow—can be done through knowing what you want (thought) and clearly setting the goal (intention) for it to happen.

ESP—Extrasensory perception—Idea popularized in the 1960s that relates to the human ability to "see" images or colors not visible with the physical eyes; "hear" sounds and tones not within audible range; or "know" the answers to questions or display skills not intellectually understood, such as a foreign language not yet studied.

feeling—Intuitive perception mode that focuses on the ability and propensity to "feel" with the physical body or emotion. Also called "clairsentience" (clear feeling).

Five-Minute "Set Your Day for Success" intention—The concept of intention distilled down to the essential elements. Used to focus the energy goals of each entire workday into five minutes of specific intention setting. The process is to (1) make your intentions as specific as possible and (2) believe in them absolutely, in other words refrain from sabotaging your intention.

Grounding—The first step in the Smart Spot process. Grounding is the human energy connection to the earth. It is the device that connects your Smart Spot to your physical body and the earth and aligns energy with intention. Energy is extended from the base of the spine into the center of the earth. It is the connecting device plus the line into the earth that comprises grounding. When you are aligned, connected, and communicating, virtually anything you intend happens. In a very real sense grounding is essential to conducting life and work with purpose and intention.

hologram—Three-dimensional imaginative structure that is the precursor to intention manifestation in the physical world. In the Smart Spot process, a viable hologram is the ideation form that occurs just prior to action.

"in the moment"—Concept of gathering all awareness from the past and future into the present moment in time.

insight—Intuitive perception mode that focuses on the ability and propensity to "know" things not known or accessible through the intellect or mental thinking.

instinct—Inborn tendency to behave in a way characteristic of a species: a natural, unlearned, predictable response to stimuli.

integrity intention—The fastest and easiest way to ensure that your own actions and those of your organization are ethical. The idea is to intend the "highest outcome for all" as part of a more specifically worded intention.

intention—The most direct route to manifesting anything. Intention is the deliberate decision to create. A grounded intention is a solid energetic form that acts as a filter for exact matches. Setting an intention is the second step in the Smart Spot process. Intention is the energy mechanism—the vehicle for momentum—that creates specific outcomes through focus and carries ideas forward for successful realization. A grand intention is a life purpose goal in business and personal life. An everyday intention is a regular life goal, such as getting to work on time or choosing an appropriate new employee.

intentional action—The implementation of an idea, plan, or solution. Acting with intention is the fourth step in the Smart Spot process—the point at which the results of the process take shape and are manifested in the physical world.

"I'm Ready" intention—Intention that affirms the intender has done everything necessary to remove doubt and create permission for energy to flow toward success.

intentional intuition—The skill that harnesses your enormous creative potential (intuition) to intuitive goals (intentions). Combining intention with intuition is the easiest method to visualize a goal and create the means and momentum to achieve it. Intentional intuition is the ability to access your intuition, and direct it through setting an effective intention to achieve what you want.

"Intuit As You Go"—Model for intentional action in which you intentionally check in with your intuition during every step in the creating process.

intuition—A natural or acquired tendency, aptitude, or talent to directly know or learn of something without the conscious use of reasoning. Accessing your creative intuition is the third step in the Smart Spot process. It is the ability to instantly know huge amounts of information and synthesize it immediately into actionable form. It is a collection of abilities ranging from keen perception (clairvoyance, clairaudience, clairsentience, and knowing) to the comprehensive proficiency to create virtually anything.

Intuition Medicine®—The science of energy according to developer Francesca McCartney, Founder and Director, Academy of Intuitive Studies and Intuition Medicine®. Intuition Medicine is the body's inner pharmacopoeia of spiritual medicine. Intuition Medicine as a science of energy is based on the body's intelligence to create an easy, practical, and enduring system for healing itself, the mind, and the spirit.

Kirlean photography—Kirlean photography is a special method used to make subtle (not seen by normal vision) energies visible. In 1939 Semyon Kirlean discovered that when half a leaf was photographed using his special camera, the missing half of the leaf would appear.

noticing—Another name for "awareness." Noticing is the quality or state of being conscious, informed, or cognizant; the intention and ability to notice behavior and subtle energy feedback to expand perception.

objectivity—Also known as neutrality. The act or process of being energetically without bias. Not attached to any particular outcome.

physical body—Your physical self, the one you know the most about, is the "you" that you bathe and dress and feed. It is your corporeal being and is comprised of your arms, legs, hips, head, and other body parts. This physical structure you think of as "you" is your "walking-around body"—the one that gets you to work and onto the tennis court and enjoys a good meal.

quantum theory—Theoretical model in the discipline of physics that unveiled a new level of reality at the beginning of the twentieth century. The quantum world is one of intrinsic uncertainty—a world of possibilities.

Research and Implement—Model for intentional action in which the big-picture solution is confirmed and expanded with analytical research and development.

synthesis—Part of creative intuition, the instantaneous sorting of all pertinent data down to its essence so that the appropriate decision is manifestly clear.

trust—Validation, both internal and external, that creates confidence in the accuracy of intuited information and right implementation.

vision statement—One example of an effective business intention. The vision statement declares the reason the organization exists and clearly communicates how it operates ethically in the world. It is the filter through which all energy in and around the organization flows and a clear, unambiguous statement of business philosophy that sets forth in as few words as possible exactly what people both inside and outside can expect from the organization.

visual—Intuitive perception mode that focuses on the ability and propensity to "see" images, pictures, movies, colors, or patterns with the physical eyes or clairvoyance (subtle energetic "sight").

visualization—A picture or movie of the intuited perception or goal. The more specific the visualization, the more accurate the perception or more successful the outcome. A visualization is a picture with specific features such as color, shape, texture, and sometimes a result or other intuited information.

Walk-Through intention—Process similar to the way athletes visualize important contests ahead of time, the Walk-Through is an intention for achievement, minimizes doubt and worry, and sets the energy for success.

"you"—Every human being is born with two bodies. The structure that you call "you" is actually a collection of parts that fall into the broad categories of your physical body and your energy body.

An Offer

The Smart Spot model is constantly in a state of re-creation. It is the quintessential product of itself. I am interested in stories you have about your own or others' experience with the process, whether or not you met with rousing success. I will use these stories to communicate key aspects of the process in my classes and workshops, and if they suggest an important change in the model, they may also be used to modify the process. If your comments are especially illustrative, I may ask your permission to mention them in the next book on the topic of intuition and personal responsibility.

Please send Smart Spot stories to me at: *feedback@dianorth.com* or contact the publisher.

To Our Readers

Red Wheel, an imprint of Red Wheel/Weiser, publishes books on topics ranging from spunky self-help, spirituality, personal growth, and relationships to women's issues and social issues. Our mission is to publish quality books that will make a difference in people's lives—how we feel about ourselves and how we relate to one another and to the world at large. We value integrity, compassion, and receptivity, both in the books we publish and in the way we do business.

Our readers are our most important resource, and we value your input, suggestions, and ideas about what you would like to see published. Please feel free to contact us, to request our latest book catalog, or to be added to our mailing list.

Red Wheel/Weiser, LLC
P.O. Box 612
York Beach, ME 03910-0612
www.redwheelweiser.com